Reading Picture Books with Infants and Toddlers

T0373628

Reading picture books with infants and toddlers facilitates their early language development, with far-reaching benefits for their later reading abilities and academic achievement.

While the importance of reading books with children aged from 3 to 5 years is widely recognised, the benefits of reading with much younger children from 0 to 3 years, who are still engaged in learning their first language, are less well understood. This book will explore the seemingly simple practice of reading picture books with infants and toddlers aged 0–3 years, from a range of perspectives. Not only do book-focused adult–child interactions support language and early literacy development in multiple ways, such interactions can also, at the same time, foster intellectual, social, emotional, and spiritual growth. By weaving together in an accessible manner the insights from several different discipline areas, this book will explain how and why reading with infants and toddlers has such power to enrich their lives.

Providing an evidence-based, theoretically informed account, *Reading Picture Books with Infants and Toddlers* supports educators, parents, and caregivers with the knowledge, skills, and motivation to provide frequent, enjoyable, and language-rich reading experiences with infants and toddlers.

Jane Torr has spent over thirty years teaching and researching in the areas of young children's language, literacy, and literary development in home and early childhood education and care settings. She has drawn on insights from systemic functional linguistic theory to support her research, which has been published in academic and professional journals.

Reading Picture Books with Infants and Toddlers

Learning Through Language

Jane Torr

Routledge
Taylor & Francis Group

LONDON AND NEW YORK

Designed cover image: © Getty Images

First published 2023
by Routledge
4 Park Square, Milton Park, Abingdon, Oxon OX14 4RN

and by Routledge
605 Third Avenue, New York, NY 10158

Routledge is an imprint of the Taylor & Francis Group, an informa business

© 2023 Jane Torr

British Library Cataloguing-in-Publication Data
A catalogue record for this book is available from the British Library

Library of Congress Cataloging-in-Publication Data
Names: Torr, Jane, author.
Title: Reading picture books with infants and toddlers : learning through language / Jane Torr.
Description: Abingdon, Oxon ; New York, NY : Routledge, 2023. | Includes bibliographical references and index. |
Identifiers: LCCN 2022041140 (print) | LCCN 2022041141 (ebook) | ISBN 9780367768928 (hardback) | ISBN 9780367768911 (paperback) | ISBN 9781003168812 (ebook)
Subjects: LCSH: Picture books for children--Educational aspects. | Reading (Early childhood)
Classification: LCC LB1140.35.P53 T68 2023 (print) | LCC LB1140.35.P53 (ebook) | DDC 372.4--dc23/eng/20221025
LC record available at https://lccn.loc.gov/2022041140
LC ebook record available at https://lccn.loc.gov/2022041141

ISBN: 978-0-367-76892-8 (hbk)
ISBN: 978-0-367-76891-1 (pbk)
ISBN: 978-1-003-16881-2 (ebk)

DOI: 10.4324/9781003168812

Typeset in Bembo
by Taylor & Francis Books

For Catherine, Alison, and Daniel

Contents

Tables

1 The Benefits of Reading with Infants and Toddlers

Stories enrich the lives of young children. Picture books introduce them to a world beyond their personal lived experience, by exposing them to captivating illustrations, interesting words, and the patterned language of different genres. When parents and educators not only read the printed words aloud, but also talk about the meanings expressed through the words and pictures, a deeper and richer type of engagement can take place. The conversations surrounding picture books forge strong relational bonds between an adult and child. These conversations provide an opportunity for mutual engagement and shared understanding. Unlike older children who can read independently, young children rely on the guidance of adults to help them access the meanings they encounter in picture books.

In addition to providing pleasure and entertainment, children's earliest experiences with picture books provide the foundations upon which their future reading skills will be built. The seemingly simple act of reading and talking about picture books with infants and toddlers is considered so significant for children's future language and literacy development that governments and professional bodies around the world actively encourage parents to read with their infant (High & Klass, 2014; Zuckerman et al., 2018). For example, the American Academy of Pediatrics, through its Reach Out and Read program, presents new parents with a complimentary picture book and advice on how to support their baby's literacy learning (Zuckerman & Augustyn, 2011; Zuckerman & Needlman, 2020). Similarly, in England and Wales, the Bookstart program gives all children under 12 months of age a picture book, together with literacy information and other resources. Similar programs are run in Ireland (O'Farrelly et al., 2018). These programs are informed by a wealth of empirical studies that show a strong association between children's earliest experiences with books and reading, and their future language and literacy development (Demir-Lira et al., 2019; Shahaeian et al., 2018).

Infants and toddlers are engaged in learning their first language(s), so it may appear premature to start reading picture books with them. Yet, as Halliday (1975; see also Halliday 2003 [1980]) has shown, one of the first symbolic "acts of meaning" produced by infants in their first year of life serves an *imaginative function*. Halliday (1975) explains the imaginative function in this way:

DOI: 10.4324/9781003168812-1

As well as moving into, taking over and exploring the universe which he finds around him, the child also uses language for creating a universe of his own, a world initially of pure sound, but which gradually turns into one of story and make-believe and let's-pretend, and ultimately into the realm of poetry and imaginative writing. This we may call the "let's pretend" function of language.

(Halliday, 1975, p. 20)

The imaginative function of language is nourished when an infant or toddler has plentiful experiences with oral story-telling, nursery rhymes, lullabies, and picture books. Such experiences facilitate the development of a rich imaginative life, while simultaneously providing many language learning opportunities and contributing to children's learning across multiple domains.

Aims of this Book

All children have the basic human right to learn to read, according to the International Literacy Association (2018), and the first steps towards the fulfilment of that right begin in the first three years of life. Parents, educators, and caregivers play a crucial role in supporting and facilitating children's development as readers. The relationship between infants' and toddlers' experiences with picture books and their future success in learning to read is complex and multifaceted. Informed by systemic functional linguistic theory (Halliday, 1994) and drawing on empirical research from different disciplines, this book has the following aims:

- to increase awareness of the relationship between infants' and toddlers' experiences with picture books and their current and future language and literacy development;
- to describe the processes involved in children's language development from birth to three years of age, and the unique role that shared reading plays in supporting this development;
- to investigate how parents and educators can facilitate children's language development, literary awareness, and learning more broadly through their talk surrounding the reading of picture books; and
- to analyse a range of picture books intended for children aged under three years in terms of their illustrations, printed text and thematic content, and their potential to support early language and literacy learning.

Shared Reading: A Definition

The term *shared reading* (sometimes referred to as *joint reading* or *interactional reading*) as it is used in this book refers specifically to the book-focused interactions that take place between an adult (parent, educator, or caregiver) and one or more children aged under three years. Three elements contribute to the overall meaning-making during shared reading of picture books. First, the adult reader contributes by reading the print aloud, talking to the child about the words and pictures, and using her voice and gestures to stimulate the child's interest, understanding and engagement. Secondly, the child participates by looking at the pictures, listening to the words read aloud, communicating through vocal, verbal, and gestural means, and physically interacting with the book by touching, patting, pointing, handling, and manipulating it.

Thirdly, the picture book itself provides a stimulus that can amuse, delight, inform and educate very young children. Picture books reveal their meanings through the interaction between the printed words and illustrations, while at the same time directly addressing the actual child and adult readers and viewers of the picture book. In picture books for children under three years, much of the meaning is conveyed through the illustrations, although the printed words are equally important. Shared reading therefore involves the complex interaction between different modes of meaning-making that run parallel to each other and intersect at various points.

Content of this Book

Chapter 1 begins with an overview of the foundational knowledge, skills, and motivations that are necessary for children to be able to learn to read after they start school. The chapter then presents empirical research showing a strong association between infants' and toddlers' earliest experiences of shared reading and their future achievement in learning to read after school entry. Chapter 2 introduces a theory of language which is also a theory of learning; systemic functional linguistic theory (SFL). As Meek (1988) explains, reading is "something with language at its core" (p. 3). This means that shared reading is most likely to be effective as a pedagogical practice if parents and educators consider what language is, how it is learnt, and the role they play in facilitating this learning.

Chapter 3 describes the potential of shared reading to facilitate children's access to the types of educational knowledge that are valued in school contexts, with implications for future reading success. Chapters 4–6 trace children's language development from birth to 18 months (Chapter 4), 18 months to two years (Chapter 5), and two to three years (Chapter 6). The role of picture books in creating contexts for learning during each phase of development is described.

Much of the research on shared reading is based on mothers' interactions with their own child. Professional early childhood educators play a crucial role in facilitating the language development of children aged under three years in group contexts. Chapter 7 explores how shared reading is enacted in Early Childhood Education and Care (ECEC) centres for children aged under three years, and the contextual factors that affect its enactment.

Chapter 8 shifts focus to consider the qualities of picture books as aesthetic artefacts and pedagogical texts in the lives of young children. The picture book serves as a catalyst for the adult–child conversations surrounding the reading, so it is important to consider the qualities of picture books intended for infants and toddlers.

Terminology

Please note that this book uses the term *infant* to refer to a child aged under two years, and *toddler* to refer to a child aged from two to three years. The adult–child talk surrounding the reading of a picture book is referred to as the *extra-textual text*. The picture book itself is the *focal text*. Unless otherwise stated, the term *picture book* refers to a commercially published picture book. The term *educator* refers to a member of staff working with children under three in an Early Childhood Education and Care (ECEC) centre. The term *caregiver* refers to other adults who have regular contact with children under three years, for example grandparents and older siblings.

Literacy and Learning to Read

Contemporary definitions of literacy involve multiple forms of meaning making, including speech, print-based and digital texts, colour, music, sound, visual images, dance, and song, all of which can be used to represent aspects of human experience. The International Literacy Association (2018) defines literacy as "The ability to identify, understand, interpret, create, compute, and communicate using visual, audible, and digital materials across disciplines and in any context". The Australian Early Years Learning Framework (Department of Education, Employment and Workplace Relations, 2009), which is a curriculum for children aged from birth to five, defines literacy as "the capacity, confidence and disposition to use language in all its forms. Literacy incorporates a range of modes of communication, including music, movement, dance, storytelling, visual arts, media and drama, as well as talking, listening, viewing, reading and writing" (p. 37).

This book focuses on one of those forms of meaning making, shared reading, and its role in supporting children's language and literacy development. To this end, this book adopts the definition of *reading* presented by Snow, Burns, and Griffin (1998); "a process of getting meaning from print, using knowledge about the written alphabet and about the sound structure of oral language for purposes of achieving understanding" (p.vi). Children's early literacy knowledge is learnt gradually and informally during the early childhood years, through observation, experimentation, and countless interactions with more experienced speakers. Participation in stories, songs, rhymes, pretend-play, and craft activities all increase young children's awareness of different forms of meaning making.

The ability to read and write skilfully and fluently is one form of literate activity that is highly valued in educational and professional contexts. Two types of processes are required for skilled and fluent reading: decoding processes and comprehending processes. These processes are sometimes referred to as constrained skills and unconstrained skills (Snow & Matthews, 2016). Decoding processes (constrained skills) involve the translation of the printed words on the page or screen into their corresponding spoken form. Comprehending processes (unconstrained skills) involve the interpretation of the words so that they make sense in the context. Skilled readers are able to apply both types of processes simultaneously to gain meaning from printed text. In order to be ready and able to learn to read and write effectively after they begin their formal schooling at the age of five or six years, young children need to arrive at school having already informally gained certain forms of knowledge and skills about print, pictures and books.

Knowledge and Skills Necessary when Learning to Read

This section outlines the types of knowledge, skills, and motivations that children need in order to be ready to learn to read after they commence their formal schooling.

Decoding Processes

Phonemic Awareness

Phonemic awareness is the understanding that each spoken word is made up of separate, individual speech sounds called phonemes. A phoneme in a particular language is recognised when paired with another word that differs from it by only one speech sound and which has a different meaning. If two rhyming words (a minimal pair) have different meanings, then the individual speech sound that distinguishes between the two words has the status of a phoneme in that language. For example, in English, the two words "cot" and "got" differ by only one speech sound (/k/ and /g/), have different meanings, and therefore they are recognised as two separate phonemes by English speakers. In the normal flow of connected speech, however, the acoustic qualities of any speech sound are influenced by the speech sounds that surround it. In the sentence "Tina caught the flu", the /t/ sound is pronounced differently depending on whether it is in the initial position (Tina) or the final position (caught) of a word. Yet readers and writers in English "hear" these two different sounds as the same phoneme /t/.

Print Concepts and Conventions

This is the understanding that print conveys meaning. It includes knowing that print is organised in certain ways on the page. In English, for example, print is read from left to right and from top to bottom.

Alphabetic Awareness

Alphabetic awareness refers to the understanding that each individual letter (grapheme) in a printed word corresponds to a specific speech sound (phoneme), and that individual speech sounds must be joined together to produce the spoken form of a word. In some languages, there is a consistent relationship between each letter and its corresponding phoneme. In English, however, there are 26 letters in the alphabet, and they represent 44 different phonemes in speech. This means that the same phoneme can be represented by two different letters (e.g. the /k/ sound in *cat* and *kite*), and the same letter can represent two different phonemes; for example the /k/ and /s/ sounds in the word *cancel*. The situation is made more complex because in English a single phoneme can also be represented by a combination of letters; for example the letters ch, sh, and th represent just one speech sound each.

Comprehending Processes

Vocabulary Knowledge

The size of a person's vocabulary refers to the number of content words a person can produce (productive or expressive vocabulary) and can understand (receptive vocabulary). Content words are "open-class" words and include nouns (referring to objects or entities), verbs (referring to actions and processes), adjectives (referring to qualities and attributes) and adverbs (referring to circumstances). Content words contrast with "closed class" words (grammatical words), which are fewer in number and contain fewer letters. Examples include pronouns (e.g. I, me, my, he, she, it, you, they) and linking words such as prepositions (e.g. in, on, by, at) and conjunctions (e.g. and, because, although).

The depth of a person's vocabulary relates to their knowledge about how words are related to each other either morphologically or thematically (Hadley & Dickinson, 2020). This includes the understanding that there is an underlying connection between words that differ in tense (jumps, jumped, jumping) and number (cat, cats). Thematic knowledge includes the understanding of taxonomies; for example that the word fruit is a superordinate term for apples and oranges, but not for carrots and potatoes.

Grammatical Knowledge

Grammatical knowledge refers to the various ways in which words may be arranged in sentences to express meaning. Spoken and written language perform complementary functions in speakers' lives, and this is reflected in the types of grammatical structures they contain to express meaning. The term *register* (sometimes referred to as *genre*) is used to describe the ways in which a speaker's or writer's choice of vocabulary and grammatical structure will differ according to the function or purpose of a piece of language. Commonly recognised registers in western cultures include narratives, recounts, and explanations.

Background Knowledge

Background knowledge refers to the way readers draw on their knowledge about the physical or social world in order to interpret the meaning of a sentence (Hirsch, 2003; Neuman et al., 2014). For example, a child who has never seen a lighthouse may be able to decode the word "lighthouse" correctly but not understand its meaning in context. All readers draw on their knowledge gained from personal experience, as well as from books, films, the internet, and conversations with other people to comprehend printed text. Intertextuality refers to the manner in which readers make connections between different texts, or across the pages of a single text, to interpret the meanings of the printed text.

A Word about Phonics

Most readers would agree that it is vitally important for children to learn to read with fluency and comprehension during their school years. How best to teach students to read has, however, been a topic of debate for decades. The debate tends to be framed in some contexts as one between proponents of a phonics-based approach as opposed to proponents of a literature-based approach.

The term phonics refers to a form of reading instruction that explicitly and systematically teaches students the connection between an individual letter, or group of letters, and the speech sound it represents. This approach works well when there is a one-to-one relationship between each letter and a single speech sound, because the word can be sounded out; for example "pat" (p + a + t = pat) and "bat" (b + a + t = bat). For many words, however, the relationship between letters and speech sounds is not straightforward, because the 26 letters of the alphabet represent 44 different speech sounds. Some words (for example, *cough, rough, through*, and *though*) cannot be sounded out. A further challenge to "sounding out" is the fact that each phoneme in a stream of speech affects the pronunciation of those around it (co-articulation). We can see this common phenomenon in the pronunciation of "fish and chips", where the "and" is normally pronounced [n]. Some of the most common words in English have irregular spellings (for example *the, was, what, people, write*), so children must learn to recognise dozens of irregularly spelt words by sight to read fluently.

Instruction in phonics is necessary but not sufficient to teach students how to read, because children also need to have sufficient knowledge of vocabulary and grammar to comprehend the words they can decode. Vocabulary knowledge is closely related to children's general knowledge about the world. Reading experts contend that both text decoding and text comprehension are equally important in learning to read (Castles, Rastle, & Nation, 2018). Neither approach is sufficient by itself to teach reading. A survey of 3,632 Australian primary school teachers (Vassallo et al., 2016) found that a large majority of teachers of grades one and two children reported using both phonics and whole-text methods to teach reading to their students.

Many children in the years prior to school learn a great deal about literacy, without being formally taught. They may recognise their own printed name, and be able to name some of the letters and numbers they recognise on car number plates and in advertisements. Reciting nursery rhymes and singing songs can enhance children's awareness that words are made up of sounds. This type of learning occurs indirectly as children go about their everyday activities. Attempting to teach children phonics prior to school age can have a negative effect on children's motivation to read (Campbell, Torr, & Cologon, 2014). The most important focus in the years prior to school is to provide young children with frequent, warm, and nurturing shared reading experiences at the same time as providing ample opportunities for craft, mark-making and drawing, arts activities, music, dance, pretend play and other forms of meaning-making. In these ways, children can build background knowledge, learn new words and concepts, and develop a love of books and reading. These experiences will stand children in good stead to be ready to learn to read in conventional terms after they start school.

Strengthening the Motivation to Learn to Read

Many factors contribute to children's motivation to learn to read, and without motivation it will be difficult for them to sustain the energy needed to keep working towards achieving success. Verhoeven and Snow (2001) stress the importance of motivation: "without some level of motivation, neither orthographic knowledge [decoding] nor comprehension strategies are likely to develop optimally" (p. 2). Seeing parents enjoying reading, having access to books and other literacy-rich materials, receiving books as gifts, and talking about the words and pictures in books, all contribute to children's positive attitudes towards reading (Baker et al., 1997). A recent empirical study found a relationship between the frequency of shared reading with infants, and children's *intrinsic* reading motivation in grade four (Demir-Lira et al., 2019). Intrinsic motivation, based on the child's inner drive to gain mastery, is more likely to succeed in encouraging students to learn to read than is extrinsic motivation in the form of rewards. Children's sense of competence and expectation that they will succeed are also likely to provide the motivation to learn to read.

Shared Reading with Infants and Toddlers and Child Language Outcomes

Age of Onset and Frequency of Shared Reading

It is often claimed that it is never too early to begin reading with infants and toddlers. Many parents begin reading to their child during their first year of life (DeBaryshe, 1993; Karrass & Braungart-Rieker, 2005), or before the child is even born (Edwards, 2014). Infants who were read to at earlier ages had stronger language skills than those for whom reading began at a later age (DeBaryshe, 1993).

To explore these findings further, Dunst et al. (2012) conducted a meta-analysis of 11 studies that included a combined total of 4,020 children, to determine whether the frequency with which parents read to their child, and the age at which they began reading to their child, were associated with child language and literacy outcomes. The age at which parents reported reading to their child ranged from 7 to 41 months, with an average age of onset of 22 months. The children's expressive and receptive language skills were measured and it was found that the children who were read to when they were younger than 12 months of age had the strongest language skills. Dunst et al. (2012) concluded that there was statistical support for the claim that "the younger the children were read to, the better were their literacy and language skills" (p. 3).

Other studies have also found that the frequency of picture book reading with infants and toddlers predicts their future language skills (Lee, 2011; Price & Kalil, 2019). An Australian longitudinal study of 2,369 infants compared the amount of book reading experienced by children when they were 20 months old and 34 months old, with their vocabulary scores at 58 months of age (Farrant & Zubrick, 2013). The researchers found that the children who had experienced less frequent book reading at the earlier ages (that is, less than 10 minutes per day) were located in the lowest 20% of vocabulary scores when tested at the age of 58 months.

More recent studies have shown that the frequency with which children are read to between the ages of two and three is associated with their academic achievement at the ages of eight and nine years (Shahaeian et al., 2018). These researchers analysed data from a longitudinal study of 4,768 Australian children and their families from varying socioeconomic backgrounds. The frequency of shared reading between two and three years of age was collected via parent report. Children's school achievement at eight and nine years of age was based on children's scores on standardised tests of language, reading and mathematics, administered nationally in Australia when children are in grade three. Statistical analyses revealed that the frequency of shared reading experienced by a child aged between two and three is both directly and indirectly associated with subsequent academic skills.

The study found that shared reading is associated with vocabulary knowledge, which predicts children's literacy and mathematical skills at school. The findings also revealed a significant direct effect of shared reading: "our results revealed a significant direct relationship between shared reading at 2 to 3 years of age and academic achievement 6 years later in reading, writing, spelling, grammar, and mathematics" (Shahaeian et al., 2018, p. 497). This study is especially noteworthy as it controlled for the many other literacy-oriented activities that occur during toddlerhood, such as music, drawing and singing, showing that shared reading is uniquely effective in facilitating children's academic achievement. Interestingly, the study also found that shared reading was particularly strongly associated with children's academic outcomes in families from lower to middle socioeconomic backgrounds.

Parent–Child Interactions during Shared Reading

More powerful evidence for the uniquely facilitative influence of shared reading on infants' and toddlers' current and future academic achievement can be found in the results of Demir-Lira et al. (2019). Unlike Shahaeian et al. (2018), who relied on parents' reports on the frequency of shared reading, Demir-Lira et al. (2019) videorecorded the naturally occurring interactions between 48 parents and their infant for 90 minutes on four separate occasions when the infant was aged 14, 18, 26, and 30 months. The parents' utterances during shared reading were coded according to their function: "reading the text, labelling or describing a picture, extending the topic, print-related talk, behavioural directives, conversational utterances, and comments" (p. 4). Additionally, the researchers determined the complexity of the parents' talk, both during shared reading and outside of shared reading. They did this by calculating the total number of unique words used by the parents (the diversity) compared with the total number of words they used. They also calculated the number of unique verbs per utterance.

Using complex statistical processes, Demir-Lira et al. (2019) found that the parents' talk during shared reading contained more diverse vocabulary and was grammatically more complex compared with their talk in other contexts. The quantity of a parent's talk to their infant or toddler during shared reading at 14, 18, 26, and 30 months significantly predicted the children's receptive vocabulary in second grade, their reading comprehension, decoding and mathematics problem solving in third grade, and their intrinsic reading motivation in fourth grade. This prediction held strong even after controlling for the parents' socioeconomic background and the quantity and qualities of their talk outside of the shared reading context.

It is also important to note what Demir-Lira et al.'s (2019) study showed did *not* relate to future reading. Neither decoding, nor the ability to solve maths calculation problems, nor external motivation to read, were predicted by infants' and toddlers' experiences of shared reading. This finding suggests that, when reading with infants and toddlers, parents are mostly concerned with achieving shared meaning and engaging in enjoyable interactions about pictures and words. This finding may relate to the fact that, even six years later, the child participants had the intrinsic motivation to read.

The data on frequency of shared reading in the home in Shahaeian et al.'s (2018) study was collected via parent report, while Demir-Lira et al.'s (2019) data comprised naturally occurring speech. The fact that the findings of the two studies support each other despite their very different methodologies adds further strength to their individual findings.

Mothers' extra-textual utterances during shared reading vary according to many factors, such as the age and interests of the child, their familiarity with the book, and their personal experiences. Senechal et al. (1995) documented how the talk of parents of 9, 17, and 27 month old infants differed during shared reading. Parents of nine month old infants labelled or described something in the pictures, and responded to the child's vocalisations. The parents of 17 month old infants drew the child's attention to something represented in a picture, described it and then asked the child a question, thus encouraging their child to engage in a conversation-like exchange.

Muhinyi and Rowe (2019) observed 44 mothers as they engaged in shared reading with their 10 month old infant. The number of words, number of questions, and type of questions produced by the mothers was calculated. The infant's engagement, affect and participation during the activity were also measured. The study found a positive association between the number of questions the mother asked, the infant's interest during shared reading, and the infant's expressive and receptive language skills measured eight months later.

Several studies have shown that shared reading provides a uniquely rich language learning context, as parents talk relatively more to their child during shared reading compared with their talk during any other activity (Soderstrom & Wittebolle, 2013). Clemens and Kegel (2021) confirmed this finding. Using automatic language processing technology, they made two day-long audio-recordings of 43 parents interacting with their infant aged between 9 and 18 months in their homes. On one of the days, the parents were asked to read picture books and play with their child, while on the second day they were asked to go about their normal activities as usual. The researchers found that the parents produced more talk during shared reading compared with talk during toy play, singing songs, mealtimes, and general caregiving.

Much of the research on mother-infant shared reading has focused on its role in facilitating vocabulary development. This is because, as Snow (2006) explains, "one of the most robust long-term predictors of good literacy outcomes *that can be measured* [emphasis added] in early childhood is vocabulary" (p. 281). Based on evidence collected on 1,073 two year old infants, and controlling for socioeconomic status, gender, ethnicity and birth order, Lee (2011) found a predictive relationship between the size of a child's vocabulary at 24 months and their language and literacy knowledge as measured from the ages of 3 to 11. In another study (Duff et al., 2015), parents were asked to assess their child's vocabulary at ages 16 and 24 months, and again when the child was five years older. The researchers found that the children's vocabulary in infancy was a statistically significant predictor of their vocabulary five years later. Such findings confirm the widely accepted view that the size of a child's vocabulary in early childhood is a reliable indicator of their language and literacy knowledge more generally, including their background knowledge about the world.

Shared Reading and Brain Development

Recent neurological research has begun to provide clues as to the impact of shared reading on the developing brains of very young children. Horowitz-Kraus and Hutton (2015) found that, when young children who have had frequent prior experiences listening to stories, hear a story, the parts of their brain associated with semantic processing become activated. Additional confirmation of the importance of shared reading can be found in a study of 47 preschoolers (Hutton et al., 2015). The researchers found that the brains of children whose home literacy environment is highly stimulating, with frequent shared reading experiences and access to books, show greater myelination of white matter in areas supporting language development. This research provides further evidence for the inextricable relationship between literary experiences, language learning, and neurological development.

Examples of Adult–Child Talk in this Book

Except where otherwise stated, the examples of mother–child and educator–child talk presented in this book were audio- or video-recorded as the adults and children went about their normal activities in the home or Early Childhood Education and Care centres. No attempt was made to intervene in these settings, as the aim was to gain insights into the qualities of the naturally occurring talk as it unfolded. The vocalisations of children under three years of age are often idiosyncratic but intelligible to the adults closest to them. In this book, the children's utterances are presented using standard English orthography, instead of phonetically, to increase the clarity for the reader.

The examples of educator–child shared readings were obtained during a funded research project investigating the language environment in Early Childhood Education and Care centres in Sydney, Australia. Ethics approval was obtained from all participants and all names have been changed to ensure the anonymity of the educators and children. The latter study has yielded significant findings about the language learning environment in Early Childhood Education and Care infant rooms, including the qualities of the educators' talk in relation to their professional qualifications (Degotardi et al., 2018; Hu et al., 2019), and educators' conceptions of, and approaches to, infant language development (Degotardi & Gill, 2019; Han & Degotardi, 2021).

Concluding Remarks

Shared reading with infants and toddlers provides them with stepping stones towards future conventional reading. The frequency and qualities of shared reading in the first three years correlate with children's future academic achievement over six years later. Shared reading with infants and toddlers is not concerned with teaching decoding skills but rather with creating enjoyable and language-rich experiences to foster a love of books and reading, while simultaneously building the foundations upon which future reading skills will be built. While this chapter has provided some generalisations about shared reading during the first years of life, it is important to remember that each individual shared reading episode between an adult and child will differ in its meaning-making. Some differences are due to features of the immediate situation, such as the time of day, place of reading, and the wellness of the participants. Children's participation is shaped by age, previous experiences with books and reading, interests and temperament. The qualities of shared reading are also shaped by more enduring influences, such as parental education, socioeconomic status, and language background, and in the case of Early Childhood Education and Care staff, professional qualifications, ratios, and group sizes.

References

Baker, L., Scher, D., & Mackler, K. (1997). Home and family influences on motivations for reading. *Educational Psychologist*, 32(2), 69–82. doi:10.1207/s15326985ep32022

Campbell, S., Torr, J., & Cologon, K. (2014). Pre-packaging preschool literacy: What drives early childhood teachers to use commercially produced phonics programs in prior to school settings. *Contemporary Issues in Early Childhood*, 15(1), 40–53. doi:10.2304/ciec.2014.15.1.40.

Castles, A., Rastle, K., & Nation, K. (2018). Ending the reading wars: Reading acquisition from novice to expert. *Psychological Science in the Public Interest*, 19(1), 5–51. doi:10.1177/1529100618772271.

Clemens, L. F., & Kegel, C. A. T. (2021). Unique contribution of shared book reading on adult–child language interaction. *Journal of Child Language*, 48(2), 373–386. doi:10.1017/S0305000920000331.

DeBaryshe, B. D. (1993). Joint picture-book reading correlates of early oral language skill. *Journal of Child Language*, 20, 455–461. doi:10.1017/S0305000900008370.

Degotardi, S., & Gill, A. (2019). Infant educators' beliefs about infant language development in long day care settings. *Early Years*, 39(1), 97–113. doi:10.1080/09575146.2017.1347607.

Degotardi, S., Torr, J., & Han, F. (2018). Infant educators' use of pedagogical questioning: Relationships with the context of interaction and educators' qualifications. *Early Education and Development*, 29(8), 1004–1018. doi:10.1080/10409289.2018.1499000.

Demir-Lira, O. E., Applebaum, L. R., Goldin-Meadow, S., & Levine, S. C. (2019). Parents' early book reading to children: Relation to children's later language and literacy outcomes controlling for other parent language input. *Developmental Science*, 22(3), e12764. doi:10.1111/desc.12764.

Department of Education, Employment and Workplace Relations. (2009). *Early years learning framework*. Australian Government.

Duff, F. J., Reen, G., Plunkett, K., & Nation, K. (2015). Do infant vocabulary skills predict school-age language and literacy outcomes? *Journal of Child Psychology and Psychiatry*, 56(8), 848–856. doi:10.1111/jepp.12378.

Dunst, C. J., Simkus, A., & Hamby, D. W. (2012). Relationship between age of onset and frequency of reading and infants' and toddlers' early language and literacy development. *Center for Early Literacy Learning Reviews*, 5(3), 1–10.

Edwards, C. M. (2014). Maternal literacy practices and toddlers' emergent literacy skills. *Journal of Early Childhood Literacy*, 14(1), 53–79. doi:10.1177/1468798412451590.

Farrant, B. M., & Zubrick, S. R. (2013). Parent–child book reading across early childhood and child vocabulary in the early school years: Findings from the Longitudinal Study of Australian Children. *First Language*, 33(3), 280–293. doi.org/10.1177/0142723713487617.

Hadley, E. B., & Dickinson, D. (2020). Measuring young children's word knowledge: A conceptual review. *Journal of Early Childhood Literacy*, 20(2), 223–251. doi:10.1177/1468798417753713

Halliday, M. A. K. (1975). *Learning how to mean*. Edward Arnold.

Halliday, M. A. K. (1994). *An introduction to functional grammar* (2nd ed.). Edward Arnold.

Halliday, M. A. K. (2003 [1980]). Three aspects of children's language development: Learning language, learning through language, learning about language. In J. J. Webster (Ed.), *The Collected Works of M. A. K. Halliday* (The language of early childhood, Volume 4) (pp. 308–326). Bloomsbury Academic.

Han, F., & Degotardi, S. (2021). Infant educators' reported conceptions of, and approaches to, infant language development: How do they relate to educator qualification level? *Early Childhood Education Journal*, 49, 259–271. doi:10.1007/s10643-020-01070-4.

High, P. C., & Klass, P. (2014). Literacy promotion: An essential component of primary care pediatric practice. *Pediatrics*, 134, 404–409. doi:10.1542/peds.2014-1384.

Hirsch, E. D. (2003). Reading comprehension requires knowledge – of words and the world. *American Educator*, Spring, 10–44.

Horowitz-Kraus, T., & Hutton, J. S. (2015). From emergent literacy to reading: How learning to read changes a child's brain. *Acta Paediatrica*, 104(7), 648–656. doi:10.1111/apa.13018.

Hu, J., Torr, J., Degotardi, S., & Han, F. (2019). Educators' use of commanding language to direct infants' behaviour: relationship to educators' qualifications and implications for language learning opportunities. *Early Years: An International Research Journal*, 39(2), 190–204. doi:10.1080/09575146.2017.1368008.

Hutton, J. S., Horowitz-Kraus, T., Mendelsohn, A. L., DeWitt, T., Holland, S. K. (2015). Home reading environment and brain activation in preschool children listening to stories. *Pediatrics*, 136(3), 466–478. doi:10.1542/peds.2015-0359.

International Literacy Association. (2018). Glossary. www.literacyworldwide.org/get-resources/literacy-glossary.

Karrass, J., & Braungart-Rieker, J. M. (2005). Effects of shared parent-infant book reading on early language acquisition. *Applied Developmental Psychology*, 26, 133–148. doi:10.1016/j.appdev.2004.12.003.

Lee, J. (2011). Size matters: Early vocabulary as a predictor of language and literacy competence. *Applied Psycholinguistics*, 32, 69–92. doi:10.1017/S0142716410000299.

Meek, M. (1988). *How texts teach what readers learn*. Thimble Press.

Muhinyi, A., & Rowe, M. L. (2019). Shared reading with preverbal infants and later language development. *Journal of Applied Developmental Psychology*, 64. doi:10.1016/j.appdev.2019.101053.

Neuman, S. B., Kaefer, T., & Pinkham, A. (2014). Building background knowledge. *The Reading Teacher*, 68(2), 145–148. www.jstor.org/stable24573715.

O'Farrelly, C., Doyle, O., Victory, G., & Palamaro-Munsell, E. (2018). Shared reading in infancy and later development: Evidence from an early intervention. *Journal of Applied Developmental Psychology*, 54, 69–83. doi:10.1016/j.appdev.2017.12.001.

Price, J., & Kalil, A. (2019). The effect of mother–child reading time on children's reading skills: Evidence from natural within-family variation. *Child Development*, 90(6), e688–e702. doi:10.1111/cdev.13137.

Senechal, M., Cornell, E. H., & Broda, L. S. (1995). Age-related differences in the organisation of parent-infant interactions during picture-book reading, *Early Childhood Research Quarterly*, 10(3), 317–337. doi:10.1016/0885-2006(95)90010–90011.

Shahaeian, A. M., Wang, C., Tucker-Drob, E., Geiger, V., Bus, A. G., & Harrison, L. J. (2018). Early shared reading, socio-economic status, and children's cognitive and school competencies: Six years of longitudinal evidence. *Scientific Studies of Reading*, 22(6), 485–502. doi:10.1080/10888438.2018.1482901.

Snow, C. E. (2006). What counts as literacy in early childhood? In K. McCartney & D. Phillips (Eds.), *Blackwell handbook of early childhood development* (pp. 274–294). Blackwell Publishing. doi:10.1002/9780470757703.ch14.

Snow, C. E., Burns, M. S., & Griffin, P. (Eds.). (1998). *Preventing reading difficulties in young children*. National Academy Press.

Snow, C. E., & Matthews, T. J. (2016). Reading and language in the early grades. *The Future of Children*, 26(2), 57–74. www.jstor.org/stable/43940581.

Soderstrom, M., & Wittebolle, K. (2013). When do caregivers talk? The influences of activity and time of day on caregiver speech and child vocalizations in two childcare environments. *Plos One*. doi:10.1371/journal.pone.0080646.

Vassallo, S., Daraganova, G., Zhang, G. Z., & Homel, J. (2016). Teaching practices in Australian primary schools. In *LSAC Annual Statistical Report* (pp. 145–170). Australian Institute of Family Studies.

Verhoeven, L. T., & Snow, C. E. (Eds.). (2001). *Literacy and motivation: Reading engagement in individuals and groups*. Routledge.

Zuckerman, B., & Augustyn, M. (2011). Books and reading: Evidence-based standard of care whose time has come. *Academic Pediatrics*, 11(1), 11–17. doi:10.1016/j.acap.2010.09.007.

Zuckerman, B., Elansary, M., & Needlman, R. (2018). Book sharing: In-home strategy to advance early child development globally. *Pediatrics*, 143(3), e20182033. doi:10.1542/peds.2018-2033.

Zuckerman, B., & Needlman, R. (2020). 30 years of Reach Out and Read: Need for a developmental perspective. *Pediatrics*, 145(6), 1–3. doi:10.1542/peds.2019-1958.

2 How Context Shapes Meaning

A Functional Theory of Language

There is now abundant evidence that reading and talking about picture books with infants and toddlers, who are yet to learn to communicate conventionally in their mother tongue, is beneficial for their language development and future growth in learning to read fluently and skilfully. Yet while there is clearly a relationship between being read to, and learning to read, the nature of the relationship is indirect and under-theorised. Language in both its spoken and written forms is integral to children's earliest experiences with picture books. To understand how shared reading is beneficial, then, it is helpful to begin by analysing what adults, infants and toddlers *do* with language during shared reading, above and beyond what they do during their other daily activities such as playing, mealtimes, and caretaking routines. To shed light on the unique pedagogical benefits of shared reading, this chapter draws on insights from a theory of language that is based on the functions language serves in the lives of speakers: systemic functional linguistic theory (SFL) (Halliday, 2007 [1988], 1994).

This chapter will provide an overview of the basic tenets of SFL, which informs much of the analysis of shared reading with infants and toddlers in the subsequent chapters. SFL has been highly influential in educational research with primary and secondary school aged children (Schleppegrell, 2004; Unsworth, 2008), but has had less influence in early childhood education contexts (Torr, 2015). Interested readers can find more detailed exegeses of systemic functional linguistic theory and its many applications in Eggins (2013), Thompson (2013), and Webster (2015).

Systemic Functional Linguistic Theory

A theory is a set of ideas or principles that provides an explanatory framework for interpreting observed phenomena. One theory of language, systemic functional linguistic (SFL) theory, formulated most prominently by Halliday (1976, 1978, 1994), posits that language is the way it is because of the functions it serves in the lives of speakers. SFL theory therefore has many advantages for those interested in researching early language and literacy development. These advantages include the following.

DOI: 10.4324/9781003168812-2

- The theory is based on observations of naturally occurring language.
- It is concerned with the meanings expressed through language.
- It gives equal consideration to interpersonal and representational meanings.
- It explains how language is systematically related to the context in which it is produced.
- It sees language as a vehicle for learning more generally.

The Metafunctions of Language

According to Halliday (1978) "language is as it is because of what it has to do" (p. 19). Language has to serve three broad abstract functions in the lives of speakers. First, it has to be about something; it has to have content (an *experiential* function). Second, it has to enable speakers to exchange meanings with each other (an *interpersonal* function). And third, it has to ensure that the content being exchanged is coherent and cohesive in relation to the situation in which it is produced (a *textual* function).

These abstract semantic functions are like different strands of meaning that are simultaneously expressed in each complete sentence in the language. In SFL, these functions of language are referred to as *metafunctions*. The prefix "meta" indicates that the functions are "above" or "beyond" what one might think of as the everyday purposes or uses of language, such as buying a cup of coffee, having a chat with a friend, or ordering a package online.

The *experiential metafunction* is the role language serves as a resource for representing experience. Through language, speakers represent their experience in terms of processes (verbal groups), the participants involved in the processes (nominal groups) and the circumstances associated with processes (adverbial groups and prepositional phrases). For example, the sentence *Jack chopped down the beanstalk* represents experience in terms of an Actor (*Jack*), a Process (*chopped down*) and a Goal (*the beanstalk*).

The *interpersonal metafunction* is the role language serves as a resource for exchanging meanings with others. Halliday (1978) points out that "Language has to express our participation, as speakers, in the speech situation; the roles we take on ourselves and impose on others." (p. 22). Language enables speakers to choose between four different speech roles, each of which serves a different conversational function. One can *give information*, by making a statement, or *demand information*, by asking a question. One can *give goods and services* by making an offer, or *demand goods and services* by issuing a command.

Each of these speech functions (stating, questioning, demanding, and offering) positions the addressee in a particular way. For example, making a statement positions the addressee as one who may acknowledge or refute; asking a question positions the addressee as one who may respond or refuse to respond; making an offer positions the addressee as one who may accept or reject, and issuing a command positions the addressee as one who may comply or refuse to do so. For example, the sentence *Jack chopped down the beanstalk* functions as a statement, in contrast to the question *did Jack chop down the beanstalk?*, or the command *chop down the beanstalk!*

The *textual metafunction* is the role language serves as a resource for organising the experiential and interpersonal meanings into stretches of cohesive text. A *text* can be defined as "any passage, spoken or written, of whatever length, that does form a unified whole" (Halliday & Hasan, 1976, p. 1). Each text has meaning in relation to other elements within the text, as well as to its immediate context, to other texts, and to the wider cultural context in which it is produced. For example, the sentence *Jack chopped down the beanstalk* is likely to be interpreted in the context of the well-known folk tale. The sentence is also likely to be interpreted in terms of one's childhood experiences associated with the tale, and the wider social and cultural contexts in which the folk tale has historically been located. Each message is organised according to the speaker's perception of what information they already share with the addressee (*Given*) and what information will be new to the addressee (*New*). The first element in the message is the *Theme*, which serves as the point of departure for the rest of the message (the *Rheme*).

One of Halliday's major insights is that each metafunction (each strand of meaning) is simultaneously encoded in each and every complete message (clause) in the language.

The sentence *Jack chopped down the beanstalk* simultaneously encodes the three different strands of meaning; it represents experience, communicates with an addressee, and presents a cohesive message.

Words and Structures: The Lexicogrammar

Halliday (1985) states that "The clause is the gateway from the semantics [metafunctions] to the grammar" (p. 66). The traditional definition of a clause is that it is a group of words that contains a finite verb. The finite element is that part of the verbal group that anchors the clause to a particular time relative to the speaker, thus making it "arguable". In the clause *Jack climbed down the beanstalk,* the finite verb *climbed* tells us that Jack's climb occurred in the past. One can agree with the statement (yes he did) or refute the statement (no he didn't).

Some verbs integrate the finite element and the verb within a single word. For example, in the clause *Jack climbed the beanstalk*, there is a finite element (did) in which the simple past tense is fused with the root meaning of the verb (climb). When seeking, rather than providing, information about Jack (*did Jack climb the beanstalk*), the finite part of the verb "*did*" serves to locate the action "climb" as occurring in the past.

In some instances, a non-finite verb will be connected to a major independent clause to extend its meaning in some way. For example, the non-finite clause *climbing the beanstalk* must be attached to a major clause for it to be meaningful (*Climbing the beanstalk, Jack heard a loud noise*). Some expressions such as exclamations (*oh my goodness*) and greetings (*happy birthday*) are referred to as minor clauses.

Language to Represent Experience: Transitivity

The experiential metafunction is realised in the lexicogrammar (the words and structures of the language) through the system of *transitivity*. The term transitivity is used to refer to "all those features of the clause which contribute to the linguistic representation of the speaker's experience" (Halliday, 1976, p. 15). Language provides speakers with a resource for representing their experience in terms of six different types of process. Each process type construes a different aspect of human experience, thus shaping the functional (semantic) roles adopted by the participants engaged in that particular process and the circumstances surrounding the process.

Material processes represent tangible, observable actions going on in the external world, such as *running, jumping, kicking,* or *swimming.* A participant who is construed linguistically as performing an action is the Actor, and the "sufferer" of the action is the Goal. In the sentence *the mouse ran up the clock* the mouse is the Actor and the clock is the Goal.

Mental processes, on the other hand, represent intangible, internal processes that can be sensed within oneself, but only inferred as occurring in other people, such as *thinking, seeing, remembering* and *loving.* There are three different types of mental process; perception (e.g. *seeing, hearing*), affection (e.g. *liking, hating*) and cognition (e.g. *knowing, wondering*).

The participant who is construed linguistically as engaging in mental processes is the Senser, and the thoughts, feelings, or perceptions that are sensed is the Phenomenon. The Senser is always a sentient being and the Phenomenon can be an entity (She thought about *her cat*) or a fact (*She thought that it was her cat*). The latter sentence is referred to as a *projection,* because the clause "it was her cat" is projected through the consciousness of the Senser ("she thought ..."). An adult's use of mental processes and projections when reading picture books with infants and toddlers is important educationally and will be discussed in later chapters.

Relational processes represent relationships between one aspect of experience and another. As Halliday (1994) puts it, "Something is said to be something else" (p. 119). The relationship between two entities may be one of *attribution,* where an entity (Carrier) is described as having a particular quality, characteristic or possession (Attribute), such as "happy" in *she is happy,* or "tall" as in *he is tall,* or "a pony" in *they have a pony.* Attributive processes are not reversible; one cannot say *happy is she,* or *tall is Tom.*

Alternatively, the relationship between one aspect of experience and another may be one of *identification.* Two different entities may be presented linguistically as being equivalent (*Susan is an artist*), or one entity may presented as being one example of a class (*A bee is an insect*). The participants in this case are Identifier and Identified. Identifying processes differ from attributive ones, because they can be reversed, for example *the artist is Susan,* and *an insect is a bee.*

In addition to these three main types of process, Halliday (1994) identifies three further types; *behavioural, verbal,* and *existential.* Behavioural processes have features that are similar in some ways to both material and mental processes. They represent physiological behaviours that are outwardly observable but may not be under conscious control (e.g. *looking, breathing, listening, laughing, crying*). The participant is construed linguistically as the Behaver.

Verbal processes represent the activity of speaking, saying, calling, questioning, asking and so on. The participant is the Sayer, the entity to whom the verbal process is addressed is the Target, and what is said is the Verbiage. Existential processes represent the fact that an entity or an action exists. The participant role is Existent. The different processes are summarised in Table 2.1, with examples of their realisations during shared reading experiences. The types of processes used by an author in the printed text of a picture book affect the interpretations of the children and adults during the shared reading, with implications for the language learning opportunities that become available.

Language to Interact with Others: Mood and Modality

Mood

The interpersonal metafunction is realised in the lexicogrammar through the systems of Mood and Modality. Mood is expressed through the ordering of the subject and finite parts of the verb in a clause. In traditional grammar, the subject of a clause is identified by asking *who* or *what* is engaged in the process. For example, in the sentence *Jack climbed the beanstalk*, one can identify the subject by asking "*who climbed the beanstalk?*" and the answer, "Jack", is the subject of the clause.

Table 2.1 Process types, key participants, and examples

Process type	Participants	Examples
Material: action event	Actor, Goal	The little girl is combing her hair. He's hiding in the cave.
Mental: perception, affection, cognition	Senser, Phenomenon	I see the sunbeams. I like those pretty flowers. I know that already.
Relational: attribution, identification	Carrier, attribute Identified, Identifier	The cave is a bit squishy. Rats are big mice.
Behavioural	Behaver	He sneezed.
Verbal	Sayer, Verbiage	She said no. What does that word say?
Existential	Existent	There's the moon. Once there was a hungry lion.

Source: Adapted from *An Introduction to Functional Grammar*, by M. A. K. Halliday, 1994, p. 143.

In a declarative clause, the subject is placed before the finite part of the verb (*Maisie flew her plane*). In an interrogative clause, however, the ordering of subject and finite is reversed. The finite element is placed before the subject (*Did Maisie fly her plane?*). In a polar (yes/no) interrogative, the information sought is either a confirmation or denial. In a WH interrogative (who, when, where, what), which seeks the name of a person, time or place, the WH word replaces the subject (*where did Maisie go?*). In an imperative, the subject (*you*) does not appear but is understood, and the finite part of the verb is the only word that is encoded (*Fly away Maisie*).

Please note that in systemic functional linguistic theory the arrow (↘) means "is realised as" and the ^ symbol refers to the ordering of the elements.

During shared reading with infants and toddlers, speech function (question, statement, command and offer) and its grammatical realisation (interrogative, declarative and imperative) play an important role in the construction of meaning. The amount of talk contributed by each participant, adult and child, contributes to the overall learning opportunities of the experience. The parent or educator contributes more talk overall, as she enacts the shared reading experience by reading the text aloud and talking about the pictures with the child or children. The relative frequency of imperatives, declaratives or inter- rogatives in the educator's talk will affect whether and if so how a child may participate during shared reading (Torr, 2020a).

Hasan (1989, 1991, 1996) explains how different types of speech function play a role in shaping young children's learning environments. In the context of questioning during shared reading with infants and toddlers, the educator's use of confirm (yes/no) questions serve a number of pedagogical functions. They position the infant as one who can confirm or deny the representational content of the educator's question, thus encouraging the infant's participation and engagement. They also allow the educator to check that she has under- stood the child's understanding (Davis & Torr, 2015; Degotardi et al., 2018), with implications for planning future learning experiences.

Table 2.2 Speech functions and their grammatical realisations

Speech function	Lexicogrammar	Example
Statement	Declarative ↘ Subject^Finite	Maisie climbed into her plane.
Yes/no question	Yes-No Interrogative ↘ Finite^Subject	Did Maisie drive her car?
WH Question	WH-Interrogative ↘ Subject^Finite	Where did Maisie fly her plane?
Command	Imperative ↘ (subject "you" implied) Finite	Fly higher and higher.
Offer	May take the form of Yes/No interrogative	Shall we read our book?

Specify questions (who, where, when, what) position the infant as one who can provide the name of a person, place, time, or entity. These "known-answer" questions encourage toddlers to verbally display their knowledge and provide opportunities for the development of naming. The pictures in picture books are symbolic representations of phenomena that a child may never have encountered in "real life", so this type of question provides them with an opportunity to encounter decontextualised knowledge in a highly supportive context. Explain questions (why, how) are rarely addressed directly to children under three years, however educators sometimes verbalise their thinking processes by stating "I wonder why that little bird flew away" in reference to the picture book text, thus indirectly inviting the child to respond (van Kleeck, 2014).

Parents and educators frequently use the imperative *look* to draw a child's attention to a salient element in an illustration, and then provide a name (*there's a steam train*). In other situations, parent and educator talk that contains a preponderance of prohibitions and imperatives is more likely to occur in group situations of two or more children (Girolametto et al., 2000) and has been shown to have a negative effect on children's engagement in a shared reading episode (Torr, 2020a).

Metaphors of Mood

Table 2.2 presents the relationship between speech function and its grammatical realisation in its most congruent or direct form. Frequently, however, speakers use their linguistic resources in metaphorical ways for a range of purposes. For example, speakers often use polar interrogatives rather than imperatives to direct a person's behaviour (*Could you please turn off the stove?*). The use of a polar interrogative rather than an imperative form implies that the addressee has some discretion as to whether or not to comply, and thus the command sounds more polite and deferential. Parents and educators often use an incongruent form of the imperative Mood to direct young children's behaviour; for example: *shall we go outside and play?* or *would you like to wriggle up closer?* Similarly, during shared reading, it is often the case that parents and educators use a declarative form rather than an interrogative to model how to make meaning from pictures (*I wonder what that is; I wonder why they went to the party*). Children as young as two years correctly interpret such metaphors of Mood as requests for information, and not as statements about the speaker's mental process.

Modality

Modality provides speakers with a resource for expressing their assessment of the possibilities and obligations involved in a particular state of affairs. Modality is realised in the grammar through a small group of expressions, including the modal auxiliaries (*can/could; shall/should; may/might; will/would; must; ought to*), adverbs (*possibly, perhaps, usually*) and projecting clauses which express possibility in a metaphorical form (*I think + clause*). A child's development of modality has implications for their ability to express a point of view and to recognise that their perspective may not be shared by others, both of which abilities are associated with their later literacy development (Hasan, 1991; Torr, 1998; Torr & Simpson, 2003). As Perkins (1983) explains, modality "may be ultimately traced back to the effect of a single fundamental human trait on language and thought. This trait [is] a basic worldview according to which it is possible to conceive of things being otherwise" (p. 162). Talking about the meanings expressed in picture books provides a particularly rich context for the exploration of the mental processes of self and other through the linguistic resources of modality.

Different Modes of Meaning Making: Spoken and Written Language

Spoken and written language are different modes of meaning making; different ways of representing experience and communicating with others (Halliday, 1985). These differences have implications for the educational benefits of shared reading with infants and toddlers, as shared reading provides young children with exposure to the patterning of written language, as expressed verbally through the familiar voice of a parent or educator.

Speech is expressed through the voice, which communicates meaning both consciously and unconsciously. In addition to their words, speakers use intonation, loudness, facial expressions and bodily gestures to add additional layers of meaning to their spoken words (Colapinto, 2021). Until the development of audiorecording devices, speech was fleeting, impermanent, and meanings could only be exchanged verbally through face to face interaction. Recent technological advances have enabled the permanent recording and analysis of human speech.

Written language, on the other hand, is communicated using graphic symbols to represent speech sounds. Writing has been used for thousands of years to provide a permanent record of events, stories, ideas, and beliefs. Writers use punctuation to express the nuances behind their words, for example exclamation marks can convey surprise, commas and full stops can signal variations in tone. Developments in digital technologies have blurred some of the boundaries between speech and writing, as emojis are frequently used to display the writer's feelings that accompany their texting.

In terms of grammar, spoken and written language vary in the proportion of content words to grammatical words they contain. Content words form an open-ended class and include nouns, verbs, adjectives, and adverbs. Content words contrast with function words such as pronouns (*I, me, my, he, she, it, you, the, an*), prepositions (*in, on, by, at*, etc) and conjunctions (*and, because, although*, etc). Halliday (1985) explains that written texts are *lexically dense* in comparison with spoken texts which are *lexically sparse*. That is, written texts contain more content words as a proportion of total words in a text, compared with spoken texts. This difference in lexical density can be seen in Example 2.1, when spoken and written language are juxtaposed during a conversation between an educator and four year old Blake reading Sleepy Book (Zolotow & Bobri, 1960).

Example 2.1

TEACHER: [*reads*] "Crickets sleep in the long meadow grass and look like the grass itself they are so still."

TEACHER: Would you sleep like that, near the grass? But crickets do. It's beautiful, isn't it? Look at its long legs. What are these here? What are these long parts here?
  They're antennas.

BLAKE: But if … if they come near me I'm going to chop 'em off.

TEACHER: Why would you chop them off?

BLAKE: Because …

TEACHER: Well, crickets don't bite, and they use these long antennas to feel and know where they're going.

In Example 2.1, the teacher reads out the printed text of the picture book, followed by a discussion about the picture. In the printed text, 53% of the total words are content words. In the teacher's extra-textual talk, 37% of the total words are content words. Halliday explains that in general lexically dense text is particularly associated with written nominalised language, especially in academic disciplines such as science: "there are a lot of things that can only be said in nominal constructions; especially in registers that have to do with the world of science and technology" (Halliday, 1985, p. 73). Shared reading offers children an early introduction to the patterns of lexically dense written text during engaging conversations with a familiar and supportive mediating adult.

The Relationship between Language and Context

One of the most important features of SFL, from an educational perspective, is the light it sheds on the relationship between language and context. According to SFL, there is a direct relationship between some elements in any material situation, and the words and structures that speakers (or writers) produce in that situation. Consider Example 2.2.

Example 2.2

> Hello. Hi. What can I get you? A long black please. That's four dollars thirty. There you go. Thank you. Thank you. Have a nice day.

Many readers will be able to "recover" some elements of this situation simply from the language itself, without needing any further contextual information. The fact that speakers can identify the context as a service encounter in a café simply from reading these few words suggests that some features of the non-linguistic setting must be inscribed in the words and structures themselves, beyond just the lexical meaning of the individual words. The politeness expressions (*hello, please, thank you, have a nice day*), the explicit naming of the commodities being exchanged (*coffee* and *dollars*), and the brevity and repetition of the speech functions involved in the exchange of goods and services allow us to recreate in our minds what was happening and who was involved.

Example 2.2 shows that there is a systematic relationship between language and context. Almost everything human beings do in the world involves language to some degree or other. The actual physical setting in which language is spoken or written is referred to as the *material situational setting* (Cloran, 1998; Hasan, 1998). Not everything in the material situational setting will be expressed in the language choices of the speakers. There are, however, some features in any situation involving language that are realised in the actual words and structures produced by the speaker or writer. The term *context of situation* refers to an abstract construct regarding three components that are realised in any situation in which language is involved. These components are as follows.

Field

The field component of the context of situation concerns the social activity that is taking place, and the subject matter it entails; "what is it that the participants are engaged in, in which the language figures as some essential component?" (Halliday & Hasan, 1989, p. 12).

This concept of social activity has been further theorised by Hasan (1995). She distinguishes between three types of social activity: action-based, relation-based, and reflection-based. An action-based social activity "reflects the fact that many of the social practices of a community are essentially of a physical nature" (Hasan, 1995, p. 251). The goals of action-based social activity are direct and lead to tangible, physical goals. For example baking a cake will result in a cake, building a house will result in a house. A relation-based social activity "is essentially an enactor of personal relationships, influencing the quality of human interactions, no matter what their nature" (Hasan, 1995, p. 252). This aspect of the field is generally undertaken in the course of some other activity. During shared reading with infants and toddlers, for example, there is likely to be some organisational talk, so that children are arranged in a position where they can sit comfortably and see the pictures.

Reflection-based social activity is entirely semiotic, such that it "becomes materially visible only through the mediation of some semiotic modality or other, language being the most of powerful of these because of its design features" (Hasan, 1995, p. 253). The goals of reflection-based activities are intangible and long-term. According to Hasan (1995), "an example of such an activity would be, say, *producing knowledge*" (p. 253). Hasan's (1995) theorisation of the concept of context of situation offers important insights when investigating the learning potential of adult–child shared reading to produce knowledge which will provide a pathway to future literacy development.

Example 2.3 is an extract from a much longer conversation between a mother and three year old Cassie. They were eating lunch while casually browsing through a travel magazine. Cassie was fascinated by one particular scene which depicted a table set with plates, cutlery, wine glasses, candles and a bottle of wine, set against a backdrop of sweeping green fields and grapevines.

Example 2.3

CASSIE: Oh. And look.
MOTHER: What's that?
CASSIE: A spoon. I've got pencils and do that. What's that? What's that?
MOTHER: That's wine. A bottle of wine.
CASSIE: Wine. People can have that bottle of wine. But girls can't have that wine.
MOTHER: [*not hearing clearly*] Girls can have that?
CASSIE: No!
MOTHER: No. Little girls can't have wine.
CASSIE: No. Big girls and boys can have that wine.
MOTHER: Boys?
CASSIE: Yeah.
MOTHER: Boys can have it?
CASSIE: Yeah.
MOTHER: Only grown up boys. Only grown up boys and girls, not little boys and girls.
CASSIE: Yeah. What's that?
MOTHER: Um … what is that?
CASSIE: A candle.
MOTHER: That's right, a candle.
CASSIE: What candles for?
MOTHER: Well, in the olden days before they had electricity … You know how we can press a switch and the light comes on?
CASSIE: Mm.
MOTHER: Well, one day they didn't have that.
CASSIE: Mm
MOTHER: They had to light candles to see by.
CASSIE: Mm.
MOTHER: And that's from those days when they had candles to see by.
CASSIE: Mm.

The field of this conversation was the action-based social activity of a mother and young child casually looking at pictures while eating their lunch together. The reflection-based activity was the verbal construal of visual images and the formulation of generalisations about experience as a result. Hasan (2006) refers to discussions that resemble Example 2.3 as *informative episodes*. She explains that "the experience of receiving sustained explicit information in emotionally supportive environments develops in these children an orientation towards decontextualised knowledge ... It becomes an aspect of their mental disposition, colouring their mental activities" (p. 174). Shared reading of picture books provides an environment in which informative episodes such as those in Example 2.3 are highly likely to occur frequently (Torr, 1997). Shared reading with infants and toddlers, during which parents and educators explicitly name and discuss the meanings of pictures, provides them with an early grounding in informative episodes as a vehicle for learning.

Tenor

The tenor component of the context of situation concerns the relationship between the participants (Halliday & Hasan, 1989). As explained by Hasan (1996), the term tenor "refers to how the speaker and addressee see themselves in relation to each other as well as in relation to the social activity at hand" (p. 46). The social distance between participants and degrees of formality affect the language choices of participants. For example, mother–child interactions will differ from doctor-patient interactions, and these differences will affect who asks questions or directs the behaviour of the other, as well as terms of address and expressions of affect. Most shared reading episodes with infants and toddlers are controlled by the parent or educator, who explicitly adopts the role of teacher, reader and questioner, and determines which aspects of the pictures will be referred to (Torr, 2020b). In accordance with early childhood principles, however, the teaching component of shared reading with infants and toddlers is characterised by positive and nurturing interactions during which children have discretion as to whether they will participate or not.

Mode

The mode component of the context of situation refers to the role language plays in the interaction. Spoken language is associated with dialogue, while written language is associated with monologue (Halliday & Hasan, 1989). The speaker's understanding of the addressee's current knowledge base will influence the degree of specificity in their language, including what is "given" knowledge (accepted as already known by the addressee), and what is "new" knowledge. Whether the activity is ancillary to or constitutive of the social action will affect the role played by language in the activity.

The relationship between the three contextual variables of field, tenor and mode, and their realisation in the lexicogrammar, is summarised in Table 2.3. Please note that the symbol ↘ means "is realised as".

Register

The term *register* (sometimes referred to as *genre*) refers to the way language varies in predictable ways according to the functions it serves in the lives of

Table 2.3 Summary of the relationship between context of situation, metafunctions, and lexicogrammar

Context of situation	Realised by (enco-ded in)	Metafunctions (meanings)	Realised by (enco-ded in)	Lexicogrammar (wording)		Expression
Field (what is going on)	↘	Experiential	↘	Transitivity Lexis (Vocabulary)	↘	Sound (phonol-ogy)
Tenor (who are taking part)	↘	Interpersonal	↘	Mood, modality, person		OR Visual (graphol-ogy)
Mode (role assigned to language)	↘	Textual	↘	The theme (theme, information, cohesion relations)		

Source: Adapted from Language, Context, and Text: Aspects of Language in a Social-semiotic Perspective, by M. A. K. Halliday & R. Hasan, 1989, p. 26.

speakers. Halliday and Hasan (1989) define register as "a configuration of meanings that are typically associated with a particular situational configuration of field, mode, and tenor" (pp. 38–39). In other words, a register is a variety of language that is typically made up of a co-occurring group of language patterns. Registers are socially recognised within all communities and cultures as they serve different purposes in society; that is, they serve "specific semiotic functions of text that have social value in the culture" (Halliday, 2002 [1997], p. 57). The ability to use the language of different disciplines, such as science, history, and literature, is central to the development of educational knowledge at school.

The Context of Situation of a Literary Text

Literary texts serve a range of purposes in human affairs, including to entertain, to express ideas about the human condition, to explore issues, to give aesthetic pleasure, to teach, to persuade, to maintain cultural traditions and strengthen religious beliefs. Literary texts have proven particularly complex to analyse in terms of context of situation, as Halliday (1977/ 2002) asserts "that of a fictional narrative is about as complex as it is possible to be" (p. 58).

There are at least two fields realised in the language of a literary text. First there is the social activity and the subject matter presented in the written text. Secondly there is the social activity involved in the reading and discussion of the subject matter of the literary text. Halliday (1977/2002) identifies a further field: "in a fictional text, the field of discourse is on two levels: the social act of narration, and the social acts that form the content of the narration" (p. 58).

Determining the tenor of a literary text is equally complex, as there are two types of relationship involved. First, there is the relationship between the represented characters in the literary text, and secondly there is the relationship between the author and the readers of the literary text.

This latter relationship has been the subject of much theoretical work in a range of disciplines. According to Hasan, in relation to tenor in a literary text:

> we need to recognise a complex interactant role: Does the author have an intended addressee? There are cases where we recognise that the reader is, in some sense, inscribed in the text: for example the nursery tales are so-called because they are primarily addressed to a specific category of readers defined by their state of maturity.
>
> (Hasan, 1996, pp. 51–52)

Reader response theorists argue that there is a particular type of reader, with certain values, attitudes, and life experiences inscribed in all literary texts (Rosenblatt, 1978).

The context of situation is even more complex when we consider shared reading as a register. The meanings in picture books are expressed through two semiotic systems, language, and visual images. The field is constructed through the interaction between the two semiotic systems within the picture book, as well as through the adult–child interactions surrounding the reading. There is the relationship between the represented characters in the picture book, and the one between the adult and child readers/viewers of the picture book. Picture books have not one but two implied readers (Chambers, 1985; Wall, 1991). The gap between the implied child reader and actual child reader affects the child's understanding of the meanings in the picture book, and the adult's mediating talk during shared reading serves to lessen this gap, although many readings of the same picture book are equally important. This is because there is too much information in the words and illustrations for children under three to construe the layers of meaning during just one reading.

The mode of a literary text also occurs at two levels. At one level, it can be seen as a monologue produced by a single author. Within a literary text, however, there are likely to be instances of other registers. Hasan (1996) explains that "what is outstanding about the appearances of these varieties in a literature work is their use as a resource for constituting the second level context, and more specifically for the realisation of the theme of the work" (p. 53). Picture books for very young children also include a variety of registers. *The Jolly Postman or Other People's Letters* (Ahlberg & Ahlberg, 1986), for example, is a narrative text about a postman delivering his mail. As he delivers each letter to the various recipients, the child reader can physically touch, open, and manipulate each letter. Each letter contains an example of a different register, including a personal letter, advertising catalogue, postcard, wedding invitation, and solicitor's letter, each of which is contained within its own addressed envelope.

Verbal Art

Most literary texts for adults express their meanings solely through language, unlike picture books where meanings are expressed through the interaction between the printed words and the visual images. It is therefore relevant to consider how the language patterns in literary registers differ from those in non-literary registers such as recounts, reports and instructional registers. This is a complex undertaking, as literary texts draw on the same basic repertoire of words and structures as other types of text. As Hasan (1971) states "there is almost no single language pattern at any level or rank which could be said to be crucially characteristic of literature" (p. 303). This raises the question as to how literary texts use language in ways that lead them to be identified as works of *verbal art*.

SFL theorists have long been interested in the linguistic patterning of literary texts. Studies by Hasan (1985, 2006) and Halliday (1997/2002) have described how literary texts "mean" the way they do. An understanding of how a literary text expresses meaning through its language choices can enrich the reader's appreciation of the aesthetic qualities and verbal artistry of the work of literature. The artistic quality of the language in literary texts is referred to as *verbal art*. Hasan (1985, 1996) has theorised that the language in literary texts differs from the language in other registers because it uses language for aesthetic purposes. She argues that the verbal art in literature can be understood in terms of the qualities of its "symbolic articulation" to enunciate the themes of the work.

The first level in Hasan's model of verbal art is *verbalisation*, which involves the basic understanding of the meaning of the words comprising the literary text. Hasan (1985) notes that "At this level the literature text is like any other text; you need to know the language to know the meanings encoded in the text" (p. 97). The second level is referred to as *symbolic articulation*. This involves foregrounding, where an expression stands out because it contrasts with a pattern that has previously been set up. According to Hasan (1985), this type of contrast serves an aesthetic function in a text. The third level is the theme of a piece of verbal art. As Hasan (1985) explains "The stratum of *theme* is the deepest level of meaning in verbal art; it is what a text is about when dissociated from the particularities of that text" (p. 97). The theme of a literary text is a generalisation about human experience.

Some picture books for young children can also be regarded as works of visual and verbal art (Kiefer, 1988; Spitz, 1999). Hasan (1985) has revealed how the language patterning of nursery rhymes draws on some of the same stylistic elements as do literary texts for adults (Simpson, 2014). As in literature for adult readers, the human condition is also the theme of nursery rhymes, folk tales and highly regarded picture books (Appleyard, 1990; Bettelheim, 1976; Rollin, 1994), albeit in a form that resonates with the particular interests, concerns, sense of humour and aesthetic awareness of children under three.

Concluding Remarks

This chapter introduced some of the basic tenets of systemic functional linguistic theory and has argued for its relevance as a tool for understanding how speakers make meaning in different contexts and for different purposes. SFL provides a theoretical framework within which to investigate the educational effects of shared reading with young children. In the following chapters, the concepts presented in this chapter assist in investigating how it is that shared reading provides infants and toddlers with unique language learning opportunities that are not available from other equally important and valuable activities and learning experiences.

References

Ahlberg, J., & Ahlberg, A. (1986). *The jolly postman and other people's letters*. Heinemann.

Appleyard, J. A. (1990). *Becoming a reader: The experience of fiction from childhood to adulthood*. Cambridge University Press.

Bettelheim, B. (1975). *The uses of enchantment: The meaning and importance of fairy tales*. Penguin.

Chambers, A. (1985). The reader in the book. In *Booktalk: Occasional writing on literature and children*. Bodley Head.

Cloran, C. (1998). Context, material situation and text. In M. Ghadessy (Ed.), *Text and context in functional linguistics* (pp. 177–218). John Benjamins Publishing Co.

Colapinto, J. (2021). *This is the voice*. Simon & Schuster.

Davis, B., & Torr, J. (2015). Educators' use of questioning as a pedagogical strategy in long day care nurseries. *Early Years: An International Research Journal*, 36(1), 1–15. doi:10.1080/09575146.2015.1087974.

Degotardi, S., Torr, J., & Han, F. (2018). Infant educators' use of pedagogical questioning: Relationships with the context of interaction and educators' qualifications. *Early Education and Development*, 29(8), 1004–1018.

Eggins, S. (2013). *An introduction to systemic functional linguistics* (2nd ed.). Bloomsbury.

Girolametto, L., Weitzman, E., Van Lieshout, R., & Duff, D. (2000). Directiveness in teachers' language input to toddlers and preschoolers in day care. *Journal of Speech, Language, and Hearing Research*, 43(5), 1101–1114.

Halliday, M. A. K. (1976). *System and function in language*. Edward Arnold.

Halliday, M. A. K. (1978). *Language as social semiotic: The social interpretation of language and meaning*. Edward Arnold.

Halliday, M. A. K. (1985). *Spoken and written language*. Deakin University Press.

Halliday, M. A. K. (1994). *An introduction to functional grammar* (2nd ed.). Edward Arnold.

Halliday, M. A. K. (2002 [1977]). Text as semantic choice in social contexts. In J. J. Webster (Ed.), *Linguistic studies of text and discourse* (pp. 3–81). (Volume 2 in the Collected Works of M. A. K. Halliday). Continuum.

Halliday, M. A. K. (2007 [1987]). Some basic concepts of educational linguistics. In J. J. Webster (Ed.), *Language and education* (pp. 342–354). (Volume 9 of the Collected Works of M. A. K. Halliday). Continuum.

Halliday, M. A. K., & Hasan, R. (1976). *Cohesion in English*. Longman.

Halliday, M. A. K., & Hasan, R. (1989). *Language, context, and text: Aspects of language in a social-semiotic perspective* (2nd ed.). Oxford University Press.

Hasan, R. (1971). Rime and reason in literature. In S. Chatman (Ed.), *Literary style: A symposium* (pp. 299–329). Oxford University Press.

Hasan, R. (1985). *Linguistics, language and verbal art.* Deakin University Press.

Hasan, R. (1989). Semantic variation and sociolinguistics. *Australian Journal of Linguistics,* 9 (2), 221–275.

Hasan, R. (1991). Questions as a mode for learning in everyday talk. In T. Le & M. McCausland (Eds.), *Language education: Interaction and development* (pp. 70–119). University of Tasmania.

Hasan, R. (1995). The conception of context in text. In P. H. Fries and M. Gregory (Eds.), *Discourse in society: Systemic functional perspective* (pp. 183–284). Ablex Publishing Corporation.

Hasan, R. (1996). On teaching literature across cultural distance. In J. E. James (Ed.), *The language-culture connection* (pp. 34–63). SEAMEO Regional Language Centre.

Hasan, R. (1998). Speaking with reference to context. In M. Ghadessy (Ed.), *Text and context in functional linguistics* (pp. 219–328). John Benjamins Publishing Co.

Hasan, R. (2006). The world in words: Semiotic mediation, tenor and ideology. In G. Williams & A. Lukin (Eds.), *Development of language: Functional perspectives on species and individuals* (pp. 158–181). Bloomsbury Publishing.

Kiefer, B. (1988). Picture books as contexts for literary, aesthetic, and real world understandings. *Language Arts,* 65(3), 260–271.

Perkins, M. R. (1983). *Modal expressions in English.* Pinter.

Rollin, L. (1994). Dreaming in public: The psychology of nursery rhyme illustration. *Children's Literature Association Quarterly,* 19(3), 105–108. doi:10.1353/chq.0.1003.

Rosenblatt, L. M. (1978). *The reader, the text, the poem: The transactional theory of the literary work.* Southern Illinois University Press.

Schickedanz, J. A., & Collins, M. F. (2012). For young children, pictures in storybooks are rarely worth a thousand words. *The Reading Teacher,* 65(8), 539–549. doi:10.1002/TRTR.01080.

Schleppegrell, M. J. (2004). *The language of schooling: A functional linguistic perspective.* Erlbaum.

Simpson, P. (2014). *Stylistics* (2nd ed). Routledge.

Spitz, E. H. (1999). *Inside picture books.* Yale University Press.

Thompson, G. (2013). *Introducing functional grammar* (3rd ed.). Bloomsbury.

Torr, J. (1997). *From child tongue to mother tongue: A case study of language development in the first two and a half years.* Monographs in Systemic Linguistics, 9. University of Nottingham.

Torr, J. (1998). The development of modality in the preschool years: Language as a vehicle for understanding possibilities and obligations in everyday life. *Functions of Language,* 5(2), 157–178.

Torr, J. (2015). Language development in early childhood: Learning how to mean. In J. J. Webster (Ed.), *The Bloomsbury companion to M. A. K. Halliday* (pp. 242–256). Bloomsbury.

Torr, J. (2020a). How "shared" is shared reading: Book-focused infant-educator interactions in long daycare centres. *Journal of Early Childhood Literacy,* 20(4), 815–838. doi:10.1177/1468798418792038.

Torr, J. (2020b). Shared reading as a practice for fostering early learning in an Early Childhood Education and Care centre: A naturalistic, comparative study of one infant's experiences with two educators. *Literacy,* 54(3), 132–142. https://doi.org/10.1111/lit.12227.

Torr, J., & Simpson, A. (2003). The emergence of grammatical metaphor: Literacy-oriented expressions in the everyday speech of young children. In A. M. Simon-Vandenbergen, M. Taverniers & L. Ravelli (Eds.), *Grammatical metaphor: Views from systemic functional linguistics* (pp. 169–184). John Benjamins.

Unsworth, L. (Ed.). (2008). *New literacies and the English curriculum*. Continuum.

van Kleeck, A. (2014). Distinguishing between casual talk and academic talk beginning in the preschool years: An important consideration for speech-language pathologists. *American Journal of Speech-Language Pathology*, 23, 724–741.

Wall, B. (1991). *The narrator's voice: The dilemma of children's fiction*. Macmillan Academic.

Webster, J. J. (Ed.). (2015). *The Bloomsbury companion to M. A. K. Halliday*. Bloomsbury.

Zolotow, C., & Bobri, V. (1960). *Sleepy book*. The World's Works.

3 Shared Reading as a Pedagogical Practice
Learning through Language

Reading picture books is universally recognised as a warm, enjoyable, and nurturing way to engage with young children (Spitz, 1999). In addition to providing positive experiences, shared reading also serves an indirect and less visible pedagogical function. Abundant empirical research shows that the amount of shared reading experienced by a child prior to 36 months of age predicts current and future language and literacy outcomes (Demir-Lira et al., 2019; Farrant & Zubrick, 2013; Muhinyi & Rowe, 2019), even after controlling for the amount of talk addressed to the child in other contexts, the home literacy environment, and the socioeconomic status of the families (Shahaeian et al., 2018). This chapter draws on examples of naturally occurring talk between parents, educators, and young children to investigate the pedagogical significance of this seemingly simple activity for children's linguistic growth and learning more generally.

A Language-Based Theory of Learning

Language is the most powerful and complex mode of meaning-making in human society. Infants begin to learn language long before they utter their first words, and parents play a central role in facilitating this learning. As neurologist Eliot (1999) explains, "When parents talk to their babies, they are activating hearing, social, emotional, and linguistic centres of the brain all at once, but their influence on language development is especially profound" (p. 367). This suggests that learning language is not simply one developmental domain among many, but rather the vehicle through which other types of learning are realised (Halliday, 2003 [1980]). Systemic functional linguistic (SFL) theory (Halliday, 1994) provides a lens through which the language produced during shared reading can be understood in terms of its potential to build the foundations for future reading.

Halliday explains the relationship between language development and other forms of learning in the following way:

> There are ... three facets to language development: learning language, learning through language, and learning about language. In a sense, and

DOI: 10.4324/9781003168812-3

from a child's point of view, these three are all the same thing. But in order to understand them properly, we need to see them apart; this will enable us to see where each comes in the overall growth and development of a child.

(Halliday, 2003 [1980], p. 308)

Halliday does not claim that all learning requires language. Children learn many things through observation, modelling, and trial and error; for example, they learn how to balance blocks on top of each other, or how water behaves when poured from one vessel to another, or how to make marks in the sand with a stick. Such modes of learning do not require language, although they may be accompanied by language. Some forms of learning can *only* be achieved through language, however, as can be seen in Example 3.1. Please note that contextual information is presented in italics in square brackets, and the actual words spoken are presented in plain text.

Example 3.1

> [*Mother and Annie, aged 20 months, are heading outdoors for a walk. As the mother opens the sliding door, Annie notices a fly pressed against the flyscreen.*]

ANNIE: [*pointing at the insect*] That! That! That!
MOTHER: [*brushing the fly away*] Oh, there's a fly.
ANNIE: [*looking at mother*] Bee … bee.
MOTHER: Looks like a bee, doesn't it? That was a fly. [*pause*] A fly. It's flown away now. [*Annie continues to stare at the place where the insect was*] We shoo flies away don't we? [*Waving her hand*] Shoo fly!

Annie initiated this brief exchange when she happened to notice an insect pressed against the screen door of her home. Using her generalised deictic (pointing) expression "that" to gain her mother's attention, and based on her current knowledge of tiny flying creatures, she identified it by giving it a name (*bee*). Annie was familiar with bees, both from her own observations in the garden but more specifically from other texts: a song about bees on a children's television program and a picture book about bees. Her mother acknowledged the validity of her daughter's interpretation on the basis of its visual similarity with a bee (*looks like a bee*), provided an alternative identification (*that was a fly*), repeated the word *fly* four times, and then used two semantically and lexically related words (*flies; flown*) in a sentence. During this fleeting exchange, Annie had the opportunity to learn what may have been a new (and difficult to pronounce) word for her (*fly*), and to gain new knowledge about insects. While bees and flies resemble each other in some ways, they are nevertheless classified as different creatures, as signified by their different names. This brief encounter encapsulated the inextricable connection between learning language and learning through language in early childhood.

A language-based theory of learning raises questions about what it is that is being learnt, and how this learning occurs. Educational linguists draw a distinction between two types of knowledge; two ways of learning and knowing about the world. The knowledge that is learnt informally through chance encounters, such as that presented in Example 3.1, is referred to as *common-sense knowledge* (Bernstein, 1975). Halliday (2007 [1988]) explains that "Common-sense knowledge is typically transmitted in the home; it tends to be spoken, non-technical, informal, without boundaries, and with room for discretion of the part of the child learner, who can take it or leave it" (p. 94).

Common-sense knowledge is different from *educational knowledge*, which is typical of the knowledge learnt by children after they commence their compulsory schooling. The manner in which educational knowledge is learnt contrasts with the learning of common-sense knowledge (Bernstein, 1975). As Halliday (2007 [1988]) explains "Educational knowledge usually comes packaged by the school; and it differs in these five ways; it is written, technical, formal, with strong boundaries and with much less discretion on the part of the learner" (p. 94). Educational knowledge is consciously built up during the many years children spend at school. Prior to school age, young children learn about their world on an ad-hoc basis during the ebb and flow of daily life. After they commence school, their existing knowledge(s) become reorganised (recontextualised) according to the protocols of different fields of knowledge such as science, history, mathematics, and so on. Each discipline uses language in its own distinctive manner, and school curricula, written by specialists, determine what children will learn and when they will learn it.

In recent decades, there has been increasing recognition of the impact of the first three years of life on children's current and future development and well-being, coinciding with increasing numbers of infants and toddlers attending Early Childhood Education and Care centres. Many governments have responded by introducing early learning frameworks to guide the work of educators (OECD, 2017). Such early learning frameworks conceptualise learning in ways that contrast both with the original notion of common-sense learning developed over 50 years ago (Bernstein, 1975) and with the organisation of educational knowledge as presented at school. Like school curricula, early learning frameworks are developed by specialists and organised according to domains of learning (e.g. communication, sense of identity, confidence and well-being). Unlike school curricula, however, learning is seen to occur during play and other activities planned by educators who observe individual children's interests and capabilities and plan learning opportunities for them.

As children become increasingly adept at using language to communicate, they seek new knowledge related to their personal experiences and observations by asking questions and presenting propositions for their parent or educator to either confirm, deny or extend upon. In Example 3.2, 36 month old Katie happens to notice her mother using an unusual type of bookmark which she had not seen before.

Example 3.2

KATIE: Mummy, do you don't miss a page when you do that?

MOTHER: Yes, that's right. You won't miss a page because that finds the page for you. [*Demonstrating*] Now, you push that down there and shut it up, and then you know where to open, you're back at the same page, see?

In Example 3.2, the mother confirms Katie's hypothesis and demonstrates its correctness with a staged demonstration of the use of the bookmark. While this interaction is informal, unplanned, initiated by the child, and tied to the here-and-now context, it nevertheless reveals the child's use of language to seek knowledge about aspects of her world as and when she encounters them.

In Example 3.3, Katie is using her linguistic resources to gain knowledge about a reality that she cannot access through her own personal experience. The nature and function of seeds in fruit can only be learnt by Katie *through* language. The casual nature of this type of early learning is evident in Example 3.3, as Katie shares her mother's attention with her younger sister, Amy, aged 21 months, leading to some fragmentation of the topic as the mother's talk shifts from one child to the other.

Example 3.3

> [*Katie, Amy and their mother are sitting at the table having a snack. Katie is playing with her doll while her mother feeds Amy who is sitting in her high chair. Some fruit is on the table.*]

KATIE: Mummy, can I have some peach?

MOTHER: Yep, you can [*handing her a peach*].

KATIE: Mummy, what is this thing inside it?

MOTHER: That's the seed. [*spooning food into Amy's mouth*] There you go, Amy. There's a bit for you.

KATIE: [*playing with her doll, and referring back to a previous conversation about the seeds in apples*] Why hasn't that got any seeds?

MOTHER: It has, see?

KATIE: Why has it got seeds?

MOTHER: They've all got a seed in the middle.

KATIE: Why?

MOTHER: Well, because the seed makes a new tree grow, if it's put in the ground, and treated properly, got the right conditions. Sit down Amy, come on sweetie, sit down please.

KATIE: Mum can I have some more peach?

MOTHER: More peach?

KATIE: Yup.

MOTHER: Alright.

KATIE: Mummy, which one is the seed?

MOTHER: [*indicating it as she slices the peach*] See the seed?

KATIE: Yup. [*long pause*] It's patterned.

MOTHER: [*several minutes pass, as the mother continues to feed the younger child and Katie plays with her doll*]

KATIE: Can I cut the seed?

MOTHER: Oh, I don't think you'll be able to cut a seed. Because a seed is very very hard.

KATIE: [*picking up knife*] How about this?

MOTHER: No, put the knife down darling, because you might hurt yourself.

In Example 3.3, much of the talk is focused on the management of the meal, especially as the younger child cannot yet feed herself independently. The mother's language is mostly ancillary to the here-and-now activity of feeding the children. Her attention slips back and forth between the two children. Interspersed with this casual pragmatic talk, however, is a different type of talk that is in sharp contrast to the rest of the conversation. The mother responds to Katie's inquiry about seeds with language that is explicit, decontextualized, and nominalised (*because the seed makes a new tree grow, if it's put in the ground, and treated properly, got the right conditions*). Such linguistic features resemble the manner in which educational knowledge is represented to children in written form during the school years.

Most children arrive at school with some knowledge about literacy, for example they may be able to sing the alphabet song, write some of the letters of their own name, and understand that print conveys meaning. After they commence school, however, they begin to learn to read in a more formal way, according to a sequence predetermined by the writers of educational materials such as phonics programs and purpose-written readers. Elements of both common-sense and educational knowledge continue to be learnt in tandem during the early years of school. In Example 3.4, students in the first grade are being inducted into the protocols of scientific inquiry, strongly supported by the encouraging talk of their teacher. Example 3.4 (Torr & Harman, 1997, p. 228) presents a fragment of the educator-student talk that occurred during a unit of work on the lifecycle of the frog.

Example 3.4

TEACHER: [*holding up a book*] What does the top of it say?

STUDENT: Contents.

TEACHER: What's the contents? [*children put up their hands*] Okay, Max, have a go.

STUDENT: That it tells us all the stuff about tadpoles and things?

TEACHER: Right, what do you mean by "stuff"?

STUDENT: Things.

TEACHER: Better word than "things". What is the book actually telling us? It's giving us something.

STUDENT: Frog lifecycles.

TEACHER: Right, but what …what's that called then, Julia?

STUDENT: Information.

TEACHER: Good girl. Information
STUDENT: Facts.
TEACHER: We could have said facts. You could have said facts or information. That's wonderful. A lovely try from the other two though. Right, don't ever give up; the right answers will come.

[*After some further discussion, the teacher continues.*]

TEACHER: What are the eggs surrounded in?
STUDENT: The … tadpoles.
TEACHER: No, what are the tadpole eggs surrounded in? We talked about that the other day … to keep them safe.
STUDENTS: Bubbles.
TEACHER: Not … well they look like bubbles, but it's more …
STUDENT: Eggs.
TEACHER: It's a jelly, right. It's like … a jelly, that protects them, around the egg, till they …
STUDENT: Bubbles … um … are squashy like that. …

Example 3.4 demonstrates the ways in which this early childhood teacher is inducting the children into the discipline of science, by using the language of common-sense knowledge while nudging them towards the more explicit, technical and nominalised language of scientific knowledge. One strategy used by this teacher is to juxtapose two words that are semantically similar but one is more technical and explicit than the other; for example *stuff* and *substances* in the sentence *The substances that are on the weeds, right? All the stuff that's stuck to the weeds, that's right.* (Torr & Harman, 1997, p. 229). She constructs lexical taxonomies by gradually shifting from common-sense language to educational language: *See how they're sort of, like, attaching themselves to that bit of dirt area? It's really their food and nutrients and sustenance in there* (p. 233). She constantly nudges the children to represent their experience of tadpoles and frogs using explicit technical language: *what do you mean by "stuff". Better word than "things".*

Early Encounters with Educational Knowledge during Shared Reading

Picture books present educational knowledge in a most accessible and condensed form, as it is supported by visual images and the explanatory talk of parents and educators. For some children, however, learning to read and write after they start school is their first experience of educational knowledge (Hasan, 2011; Williams, 2001). While the concept of educational knowledge is generally associated with children's learning as they move through the grades at school, recent research suggest that educational knowledge has its origins in children's earliest experience with picture books in the first three years of life. This is because early shared reading is predictive of their academic success well into the primary school age ranges. In one research study, for example, Shahaeian et al. (2018) studied the development of 4,768 children over a six year period and found that there is "a significant direct relationship between shared reading at 2 to 3 years of age and academic achievement six years later in reading, writing, spelling, grammar, and mathematics" (p. 497). Using a different methodology, Demir-Lira et al. (2019) studied the development of 48 infants aged from 14 to 30 months, and found that "the quantity of parent book reading predicts important child language and literacy outcomes, controlling for parent language input outside of the reading context, the child's own contribution, overall child talk, and parent SES" (p. 1).

In the light of such powerful findings, it is worthwhile to consider what it is about the experience of shared reading that provides infants and toddlers, many of whom are still learning their first language(s), with a pathway to future success in the development of educational knowledge. Shared reading is qualitatively different from all other learning experiences in the life of a young child. This is because shared reading is entirely a multimodal semiotic process; a process of visual and verbal meaning-making that can only be construed, made sense of, and interpreted by young children through the mediating verbal guidance of an adult.

During shared reading, infants and toddlers are apprenticed into the conscious construal of explicit educational knowledge in developmentally appropriate, language rich and emotionally supportive ways. The child's experience of educational knowledge is mediated by the adult and explicitly articulated in ways that are appropriate for each individual child's level of understanding. Educational knowledge thus has its origins in the practice of shared reading with infants and toddlers. This confluence of common-sense and educational knowledge was noted by Halliday (2007 [1988]) who long ago wrote that "before children ever go into school their parents read to them out of books, and some children learn to read quite a lot all by themselves" (p. 369).

As they gain greater exposure to picture books of different kinds, young children come to understand how picture books work as visual and verbal texts, and approach each new picture book with some expectations about its content and function. The following section presents some of the concepts that children under three years have the opportunity to learn from frequent shared reading of picture books.

Concept 1: Pictures Are Aesthetic Objects

Shared reading provides children with access to a wide variety of artistic styles and content, providing them with the opportunity to develop further their own preferences and aesthetic awareness. From early in life, infants express their preference for some pictures rather than others, demonstrating an early expression of aesthetic awareness. Portera (2020) defines aesthetic capacity as "being able to engage with perceptual aspects of the world where, at the very least, attentional resources, emotions, energy expenditure, and a selective judgment (even implicit) come into play. All this is generally associated with pleasure/displeasure" (p. 305). When infants gain control over what they look at, they gaze intently at some visual images in preference to others, as presented in Examples 3.5 and 3.6.

Example 3.5

> Eight week old Ariana was placed on a rug on the floor during "tummy time". She was surrounded by toys and some hardcover picture books propped open so that she could look at them. She showed a definite preference for one picture of a blue bird. She ignored the other pictures and became animated when she saw the bird picture.

Example 3.6

> When three month old Alex was lying on his changing table, he noticed a box of nappies nearby on which he could see a picture of a baby's face. He gazed at the picture while ignoring other pictures in his visual field. Each time he had his nappy changed, he looked at the picture of the baby, smiled and moved his arms and legs as if trying to touch the picture.

Unlike adults who can reflect on their aesthetic reactions to works of art, infants and toddlers communicate their aesthetic pleasure in response to certain pictures by smiling, gazing, touching, patting, vocalising and/or moving towards a picture. Pictures also figure strongly in the early phases of language development. One of the first acts of meaning produced by Halliday's ten month old son Nigel was glossed by Halliday (1975) as "nice to see you and shall we look at this picture together" (p. 23). Torr (1997) found that most of her daughter's earliest pro-tolanguage signs were related to pictures in one way or another. On rare occasions, adults would themselves refer to the aesthetic qualities of pictures. Please see Examples 3.7 and 3.8.

Example 3.7

MOTHER: [*referring to pictures in a picture book*] They're water lilies. They're
    plants that grow in the water. They're pretty, aren't they?
CASSIE: A pink. Why they pink? [*pretending*] Pick! I pick one.

Example 3.8

MOTHER: [*referring to picture of a sunset in a picture book*] You know what I like
    about this page?
ALEX: What?
MOTHER: The pretty colours. They're very sleepy colours I think.
ALEX: Mm.
MOTHER: Purple and orange. And it makes me feel sleepy.

Concept 2: Pictures Convey Meaning

It is sometimes assumed that the meanings in pictures are transparent to young children, yet children need to learn how to "read" pictures just as they learn to read printed text (Schickedanz & Collins, 2012). While individual pictures in the environment (e.g. hanging on the wall, in advertisements, or on packets) can be enjoyed aesthetically, their meanings as semiotic texts can only be construed through interactions with others. This is because the pictures in picture books create meaning through the interaction between the picture and the print on each individual page, and across all the pages of the book.

During shared reading, infants and toddlers have the opportunity to explore the meanings in pictures when interacting with an adult who provides guidance on how pictures "mean" in the context of the picture book as a whole. The ability to understand and produce information visually in diagrams, maps and tables plays an important role in future access to educational knowledge and must be learnt. As DeLoache et al. (2003) explain, "Pictorial competence, which refers to the many factors involved in perceiving, interpreting, understanding, and using pictures, develops gradually over the first few years of life" (p. 114).

Some supposedly simple "baby books" depict objects thought to be familiar to infants and therefore easily recognisable by them, such as baby bottles, food, toys, and clothing. However, such two dimensional pictures do not actually resemble the three dimensional real-life object they are intended to represent. For example the pictures in so-called labelling books depict familiar objects as new, clean and unused, unlike the real objects that are used and handled by children (Kummerling-Meibauer & Meibauer, 2005). As explained by Golden and Gerber (1990), all pictures in picture books represent concepts or interpretations of objects, not the actual objects themselves; "the word bird, for example, evokes the idea of a bird rather than the actual object" (p. 205). This means that identifying and naming an object in a picture or photograph requires an act of interpretation on the part of the child.

In picture books for infants and toddlers, the illustrations tend to take precedence over the relatively the small amount of printed text. This places the emphasis on the illustrations as the primary medium through which meanings are realised. A classic example is *Rosie's Walk* (Hutchins, 2009 [1967]), in which the full meaning of the narrative is represented entirely in the illustrations. The printed text does not refer at all to the dramatic events unfolding in the pictures, just as the main character Rosie the hen remains oblivious to the attempts of the fox to capture her. Many illustrators of picture books for young children include additional features beyond those that are specifically necessary to follow the basic plotline (Martinez & Harmon, 2012). These additional details create humour and interest, and become talking points between parents, educators and children.

Children begin to learn how to read pictures during their earliest encounters with picture books. Studies have repeatedly shown how mothers first begin to interact with their child during shared reading by asking them to point to and/ or name the objects or entities depicted in the illustrations of picture books. Example 3.7 is typical of this kind of interaction. In Example 3.7, the mother and 19.5 month old Lucy are sitting together at the table. In front of them is a random pile of picture books of varying lengths and quality. Lucy chooses the *Tawny Scrawny Lion* (Jackson & Tenggren, 1980 [1952]) and hands it to her mother.

Example 3.9

MOTHER: [*opening to the title page*] Do you know what these animals are?
LUCY: [?duck]
MOTHER: Where's the lion?
LUCY: [*pointing at the monkey*] There.
MOTHER: Is that a lion?
LUCY: Yes.
MOTHER: No, that's a monkey. Monkey.
LUCY: Yeah.
MOTHER: [*pointing to animals in a sequence*] Rabbit.
LUCY: [*pointing*] There.
MOTHER: [*pointing*] Lion.
LUCY: There.
MOTHER: [*pointing*] What's that one?
LUCY: There.
MOTHER: Kangaroo.
LUCY: Roo.
MOTHER: [*pointing*] Zebra.
LUCY: Zebra.

The title page of this picture book depicts six animals forming a semicircle around the printed title of the book. While the pictures of five of the six animals are represented in a realistic manner, the sixth animal, a rabbit, is depicted in a human-like way wearing clothes, standing on two legs and carrying a basket. Lucy had not seen these animals in real life, so had no way of identifying them from personal experience. This means that Lucy is being asked to name a visual interpretation of each animal, a symbol. Lucy's responses in Example 3.7 suggest that she has begun to understand that entities depicted in pictures can be named.

The illustrators of picture books convey their meanings visually through the use of line, colour, framing, placement of characters relative to each other, and other visual elements. Shared reading of picture books provides plentiful opportunities for parents and educators to explain the meanings of the marks and lines in pictures that are used conventionally to represent action, movement, speech and thought (Giorgis et al., 1999; Lewis, 2001). For example, on several pages of *Maisy's Plane* (Cousins, 2014), the movement and direction of the plane is depicted in the form of white lines crossing the double page spread. As the educator of 21 month old Charlie read and talked about the pictures, the educator used her finger to trace the trajectory of the plane while explaining "Look at Maisy's aeroplane. Goes up and up, up into the sky" (Torr, 2020, p. 137).

As children gain more experience construing the meanings of the pictures in picture books, they use their language as a means of interpreting symbols, as can be seen in the conversation between four year old Alexandra and her educator in example 3.10 (Torr & Scott, 2006, p. 162).

Example 3.10

> [*Alexandra and her educator are reading* Sleepy Book *(Zolotow & Bobri, 1958) together. On one page, a seal is depicted asleep in the foreground, and in the background is a series of curved lines to represent the rays of the sun reflected on the water.*]

ALEXANDRA: What's that?
EDUCATOR: I think it's the sun setting maybe.
ALEXANDRA: Yeah, cause I think those … um … things go along the sun.
ALEXANDRA: Yeah, it's a reflection, isn't it?

Concept 3: Picture Books Contain New and Interesting Words

Shared reading exposes children to new and unfamiliar vocabulary. Empirical research has confirmed that picture books contain more unusual vocabulary than occurs in other situations. Massaro (2015) compared the number and type of words in 112 picture books with the number and type of words in the speech of adults addressed to children and other adults. He found more different and rare words (types) in the picture books, compared with those in the adults' speech. Other research supports this finding. Montag et al. (2015) studied a corpus of a 100 well-known children's picture books recommended by librarians as being appropriate for children aged from birth to five. Montag et al. (2015) found that the picture books contained more unique word types than were found in the parents' speech to their child.

In order to learn new words, children have to hear them in context and develop what Christ and Wang (2010) refer to as "word consciousness" (p. 85); that is, an interest in and awareness of the meanings of new words and how they relate to other words. A child's word consciousness is most likely to develop when they are interested in the subject matter being discussed. When they encounter a new word in a picture book during shared reading, they have the dual interactive support of the adult guide and the visual images to assist them to construe the meaning of the new word in context. Example 3.11 presents an example in which four year old Karen recognises and seeks to understand what is, for her, a new word she just encountered in the picture book (Torr & Scott, 2006, p. 163).

Example 3.11

KAREN: Lullaby? What's a lullaby?
MOTHER: Like "Rock a Bye Baby". You know, a soft song that makes you fall asleep. They're musicians so they play music, so they play soft sleepy music instead of happy dance party music. So they say it's time for bed.

Concept 4: Picture Books Relate to One's Own Life

During the years prior to school, children gradually come to understand that their thoughts, feelings and perceptions can only be accessed by other people if they verbally articulate them. This understanding is important for future reading and writing development. When producing written text, the writer needs to distinguish between information that the addressee already knows, or is likely to know, and information that is new to the addressee and therefore must be explicitly articulated in the written text. The adult–child talk during shared reading provides multiple opportunities for children to gain experience in inferring the mental processes of others and reflecting on their own thoughts and feelings. In Example 3.12, Annie (25 months) and her mother are reading *Humbert, Mr Firkin and the Lord Mayor of London* (Burningham, 1965).

Example 3.12

MOTHER: Look. This one [*a horse*] is having his teeth brushed. See the big toothbrush?
ANNIE: Oh.
MOTHER: Did you know horses brush their teeth?
ANNIE: [*nodding*] Yeah, did.
MOTHER: Yeah, you do, don't you?
ANNIE: [*shaking her head*] A paste.
MOTHER: Not with toothpaste, no …
ANNIE: [*nodding*] A me paste!
MOTHER: [*laughing*] Yes you do use paste. Yes, toothpaste.
ANNIE: [*pointing*] There Humbert.

Parents and educators often preface their questions and comments during shared reading by referring to their own mental processes (*I think, I know, I wonder*), thus making their thinking "visible" to the infant or toddler (Van Kleeck et al., 1996; Torr, 2020). Similarly, they may ask the child questions in ways that position the child as the knower and thinker, for example in Example 3.12 (*did you know horses brush their teeth*). Such references to mental processes provide young children with some experience with the discourse features of academic inquiry. An important prerequisite for the achievement of educational knowledge is the ability to recognise that one's perspective may not be shared by others (Hasan, 2011;

Williams, 1999), and to frame one's talk about various states of affairs on the basis of this recognition.

Picture books provide young children with opportunities to develop and articulate their understanding of their own emotions and to feel empathy for others (Prior et al., 2012; Spitz, 1999). As explained by Kucirkova (2019), some perspectives on empathy state that "empathy involves a recognition of another person's feelings and a response to it" (p. 4). A common feature of narrative picture books is to represent a character (human or animal) who has experienced a loss (a toy or a friend), or who has suffered an injury. Picture books depict the emotions of the characters in the illustrations, the printed words, and/or both modes. When reading picture books that represent a character experiencing sadness, loss or fear, the adult reader often takes the opportunity to express empathy for the character by making a text-to- life connection as in example 3.13.

Example 3.13

ANNIE: Oh look.
MOTHER: Oh, he doesn't look happy at all, does he?
ANNIE: Cry.
MOTHER: Crying, because he fell. He had a big fall. Do you cry when you have a big fall?
ANNIE: [*shaking head*] No.
MOTHER: Some people cry when they have a big fall.
ANNIE: Look.
MOTHER: Poor Donald. Had a big fall. Still, don't worry, because he soon feels better. Look, he's happy again.
ANNIE: Yeah. Look, look, look. Finished.

It is thought that children's connections between the events in picture books and their own lives facilitate their motivation to engage with books and reading (Elster, 1995; Sipe 2000), and assist them to identify the meanings in literary texts (Lehr, 1990).

Concept 5: All Picture Books have Features in Common

The term *intertextuality*, as used in the context of shared reading with young children, refers to the way parents, educators and children themselves draw on their experiences with other texts to construe the meanings in a focal text. By making intertextual connections, children are moving beyond the frame of the focal text. Please see Example 3.14.

Example 3.14

MOTHER: Mm. Where's the bear?
ANNIE: [*shaking head*] Not there.

MOTHER: Yes, there is. Where's the bear? [*pause*] There is a bear there.

ANNIE: [*points*] There!

MOTHER: That's right!

ANNIE: bzzzzzzzz [*making bee sound and moving finger to represent a bee in flight*].

MOTHER: That's right! Are you pretending to be a bee, like in the other book? With the bear?

ANNIE: Yeah.

MOTHER: Mm. It looks a bit different to the other bear. It does look different to the honey bear.

ANNIE: Bear. Bear.

MOTHER: To ... to the bear in the Big Honey Hunt book.

ANNIE: Yeah.

Example 3.14 suggests that the child is making a connection between the representation of a bear in one picture book and its representation in another one of her picture books *The Big Honey Hunt* (Berenstain & Berenstain, 1962). The contentious relationship between bears and honey is a common motif in western cultures and has been represented in countless children's picture books, cartoons, videos, and other popular texts, indicating the pervasiveness of popular culture in the lives of young children.

Text-to-text connections become more detailed as children gain greater experience with picture books and become more verbally adept, as can be seen in Examples 3.15 (Torr, 2007, p. 87) and 3.16 (ibid., p. 88) with children aged from three to four years while reading *Sleepy Book* (Zolotow & Bobri, 1958).

Example 3.15

EDUCATOR: [*reading*] "Tortoises sleep in their shells and no one would know a tortoise was there".

LUKE: Well, I saw ... um ... Rupert Bear. But Little Bear should be on and I saw a turtle and he thought it was a rock but it ... it was moving ... slowly.

EDUCATOR: So they know that it wasn't a rock ...if it was moving.

LUKE: Yeah and ... and he's a rock and he was a turtle. And he thought it was like that.

Example 3.16

MOTHER: [*reading*] "Spiders when they sleep are like small ink spots in the middle of their lacy webs".

JACKSON: And there's a spider.

MOTHER: We read a story about a spider a little while ago, didn't we?

JACKSON: What was it called?

MOTHER: Was it Arania?

JACKSON: Yeah.
MOTHER: And what happened to her?
JACKSON: We've still got it.
MOTHER: Yeah. What happened to that spider?
JACKSON: Couldn't make his web. But, ah, his corners came loose.

Picture Books and Decontextualised Language

The term *decontextualised* refers to language that does not rely on features in the immediate environment for its interpretation. In a longitudinal study of 42 toddlers that commenced when the children were 30 months of age, Uccelli et al. (2019) found an association between children's use of decontextualised language and their academic achievement over ten years later. Shared reading is an activity that is not dependent on the material setting for its meaning-making. This is because the experiential content of the picture book (field) and the relationship between the participants (tenor) do not change if the material setting changes. Another opportunity to experience decontextualised knowledge can be found in the content of picture books themselves. Books present concepts that have no tangible existence in the real world; for example, mice who can pilot aeroplanes (Cousins, 2014), pigs who sing (Boynton, 2011 [1984]), and colourful sheep who read, juggle, ride on skateboards and stand on the moon (Fox & Horacek, 2004).

Organisation of Educational Knowledge

The ability to sustain a topic over stretches of text is a fundamental feature of educational knowledge. Picture books present knowledge in a systematic way. The content of the picture book guides and shapes the surrounding adult–child talk, thus providing young children with an experience of topic-centred talk (Michaels, 1981).

How information is organised in picture books depends on whether the book is primarily narrative or informational. Narrative picture books create cohesion by focusing on the actions of one or more individual characters as they take place in a sequence over time. Informational picture books create cohesion by organising knowledge according to themes. For example, animals may be categorised according to whether they are farm animals, wild animals, baby animals, pet animals or extinct animals, thus providing young children with early textual experiences that foreshadow the organisation of knowledge in school, where knowledge is divided into different content areas such as science, history, and geography (see Example 3.17).

Educators' talk around narratives tends to focus on features of the plot and the thoughts and feelings of the main character, while the talk around informational texts tends to lead to generalisations about whole classes of entities (Torr & Clugston, 1999).

Example 3.17

[*Freddy, aged 18 months, and three other children are gathered around an educator who is sitting at a table with two children who are eating. The teacher has some books in front of her, and the children bring her some more books. She opens an informational book about sea animals. It is a touch-and-feel book, with different textures for the children to touch.*]

FREDDY: A book. A book.
EDUCATOR: What's this?
FREDDY: ?penguin.
EDUCATOR: Penguin [*reading*] A penguin is a bird but cannot fly.
FREDDY: Bumpy [*pointing and touching the book*]
EDUCATOR: [*reading*] He dives in the ocean underneath the sky.
OTHER CHILD: Sky.
TEACHER: Yeah, push on it, pat the penguin. Pat pat pat.
OTHER CHILD: [*touching picture in book*] Pat, pat.
TEACHER: Pat pat What's that? (to other child)
EDUCATOR: [*reading*] Mamma bear and baby bear catch a fish that they can share.

[*addressing other child and referring to picture of bear*] Pat Mamma bear!

OTHER CHILD: Mummy?
EDUCATOR: Mummy bear? Turn the page. [*reading*] The zebra has stripes that are black and white. Touch the zebra. [*children touch the picture of the zebra*] Gentle with the book. Gentle hands.

Implications for Future Reading Development

Shared reading at a young age orients children to some types of meaning that are characteristic of educational knowledge. Background knowledge is vitally important for children to be able to learn to read effectively after they commence school. Parents and educators can build children's background knowledge by choosing to read a range of picture books on different topics, thus exposing young children to the patterning of different registers. Parents and educators can encourage the participation of infants and toddlers by asking questions, communicating their own pleasure and enthusiasm, and allowing children to develop their aesthetic preferences and interests by providing a wide range of picture books. By juxtaposing the printed text read aloud, the spoken interactions surrounding the read text, and the talk about words and pictures, children gain knowledge about how different modes of expression can combine during multimodal meaning making.

Concluding Remarks

Shared reading provides unique language learning opportunities during which elements of both common-sense and educational knowledge are intertwined.

Halliday (2007 [1988]) explains that "These two aspects of children's learning experience, common-sense learning and educational learning, are not of course insulated one from the other: there is continuity between the two" (p. 368).

References

Berenstain, S., & Berenstain, J. (1962). *The big honey hunt.* Beginner Books.

Bernstein, B. (1975). *Class, codes and control: Towards a theory of educational transmissions* (volume 3). Routledge and Kegan Paul.

Boynton, S. (2011 [1984]). *Moo, baa, la la la!* Little Simon.

Burningham, J. (1965). *Humbert, Mr Firkin and the Lord Mayor of London.* Jonathan Cape.

Christ, T., & Wang, C. (2010). Bridging the vocabulary gap: What research tells us about vocabulary instruction in early childhood. *Young Children*, July.

Cousins, L. (2014). *Maisy's Plane.* Walker Books.

DeLoache, J. S., Pierrouttsakos, S. L., & Uttal, D. H. (2003). The origins of pictorial competence. *Current Directions in Psychological Science*, 12(4), 114–118. www.jstor.org/stable/20182855.

Demir-Lira, O. E., Applebaum, L. R., Goldin-Meadow, S., & Levine, S. C. (2019). Parents' early book reading to children: Relation to children's later language and literacy outcomes controlling for other parent language input. *Developmental Science*, 22 (3), e12764. doi:10.1111/desc.12764.

Eliot, L. (1999). *Early intelligence: How the mind and brain develop in the first five years of life.* Penguin Books.

Elster, C. (1995). Importations in preschoolers' emergent reading. *Journal of Reading Behavior*, 27(1), 65–85.

Farrant, B. M., & Zubrick, S. R. (2013). Parent–child book reading across early childhood and child vocabulary in the early school years: Findings from the Longitudinal Study of Australian Children. *First Language*, 33(3), 280–293. doi:10.1177/0142723713487617.

Fox, M., & Horacek, J. (2004). *Where is the green sheep?* Penguin.

Giorgis, C., Johnson, N. J., Bonomo, A., Colbert, C., Connor, A., Kauffman, G., & Kulesza, D. (1999). Children's books: Visual literacy. *The Reading Teacher*, 53(2), 146–153. www.jstor.org/stable/20204765.

Golden, J. M., & Gerber, A. (1990). A semiotic perspective of text: The picture book story event. *Journal of Reading Behavior*, 12(3), 203–2019.

Halliday, M. A. K. (1975). *Learning how to mean.* Edward Arnold.

Halliday, M. A. K. (1994). *An introduction to functional grammar* (2nd ed.). Edward Arnold.

Halliday, M. A. K. (2003 [1980]). Three aspects of children's language development: Learning language, learning through language, learning about language. In J. J. Webster (Ed.), *The collected works of M. A. K. Halliday* (The language of early childhood, Volume 4) (pp. 308–326). Bloomsbury Academic.

Halliday, M. A. K. (2007 [1988]). Language and socialisation: Home and school. In J. J. Webster (Ed.), *The collected works of M. A. K. Halliday* (Language and education, Volume 9) (pp. 81–96). Continuum.

Hasan, R. (2011). Modes of learning, modes of teaching: Semiotic mediation and knowledge. In J. J. Webster (Ed.), *The collected works of Ruqaiya Hasan* (pp. 48–72). Volume 3. Equinox.

Hutchins, P. (2009 [1967]). *Rosie's walk.* Penguin Random House.

Jackson, K., & Tenggren, G. (1980 [1952]). *Tawny Scrawny Lion.* Random House.

Kummerling-Meibauer, B., & Meibauer, J. (2005). First pictures, early concepts: Early concept books. *The Lion and the Unicorn*, 29(3), 324–347. doi:10.1353/uni.2005.0039.

Kucirkova, N. (2019). How could children's storybooks promote empathy? A conceptual framework based on developmental psychology and literary theory. *Frontiers in Psychology*, 10, 121, 1–15. doi:10.3389/fpsyg.2019.00121.

Lehr, S. (1990). Literature and the construction of meaning: The preschool child's developing sense of theme. *Journal of Research in Childhood Education*, 5(1), 37–46.

Lewis, D. (2001). *Reading contemporary picture books: Picturing text.* Routledge.

Martinez, M., & Harmon, J. M. (2012). Picture/text relationships: An investigation of literary elements in picturebooks. *Literacy Research and Instruction*, 51(4), 323–343. doi:10.1080/19388071.2012.695856.

Massaro, D. W. (2015). Two different communication genres and implications for vocabulary development and learning to read. *Journal of Literacy Research*, 47(4), 505–527. doi:10.1177/1086296X15627528.

Michaels, S. (1981). "Sharing time": Children's narrative styles and differential access to literacy. *Language in Society*, 10(3), 423–442. www.jstor.org/stable/4167263.

Montag, J., L., Jones, M. N., & Smith, L. B. (2015). The words children hear: Picture books and the statistics for language learning. *Psychological Science*, 26(9), 1489–1496. doi:10.1177/0956797615594361.

Muhinyi, A., & Rowe, M. L. (2019). Shared reading with preverbal infants and later language development. *Journal of Applied Developmental Psychology*, 64. doi:10.1016/j.appdev.2019.101053.

OECD. (2017). *Starting strong 2017: Key OECD indicators on early childhood education and care.* OECD Publishing. doi:10.1787/9789264276116-en.

Portera, M. (2020). Babies rule! Niches, scaffoldings and the development of an aesthetic capacity in humans. *British Journal of Aesthetics*, 60(3), 299–314. doi:10.1093/aesthj/ayz064.

Prior, L. A., Willson, A., & Martinez, M. (2012). Picture this: Visual literacy as a pathway to character understanding. *The Reading Teacher*, 66(3), 195–206. www.jstor.org/stable/23321279.

Schickedanz, J. A., & Collins, M. F. (2012). For young children, pictures in storybooks are rarely worth a thousand words. *The Reading Teacher*, 65(8), 539–549. doi:10.1002/TRTR.01080.

Shahaeian, A. M., Wang, C., Tucker-Drob, E., Geiger, V., Bus, A. G., & Harrison, L. J. (2018). Early shared reading, socio-economic status, and children's cognitive and school competencies: Six years of longitudinal evidence. *Scientific Studies of Reading*, 22(6), 485–502. doi:10.1080/10888438.2018.1482901.

Sipe, L. R. (2000). The construction of literary understandings by 1st- and 2nd-graders in oral response to picture storybook read-alouds. *Reading Research Quarterly*, 35(2), 252–281.

Spitz, E. H. (1999). *Inside picture books.* Yale University Press.

Torr, J. (1997). *From child tongue to mother tongue: A case study of language development in the first two and a half years.* Monographs in Systemic Linguistics, 9. University of Nottingham.

Torr, J. (2007). The pleasure of recognition: Intertextuality in the talk of preschoolers during shared reading with mothers and teachers. *Early Years: An International Journal of Research and Development*, 27(1), 77–91. doi:10.1080/09575140601135163.

Torr, J. (2020). Shared reading as a practice for fostering early learning in an Early Childhood Education and Care centre: A naturalistic, comparative study of one infant's experiences with two educators. *Literacy*, 132–142. doi:10.1111/lit.12227.

Torr, J., & Clugston, L. (1999). A comparison between narrative and informational picture books as a context for reasoning between caregivers and 4-yearold children. *Early Child Development and Care*, 159(1), 25–41. doi:10.1080/030044399159104.

Torr, J., & Harman, J. (1997). Literacy and the language of science in Year 1 classrooms: Implications for children's learning. *Australian Journal of Language and Literacy*, 20(3), 222–237.

Torr, J., & Scott, C. (2006). Learning "special words": Technical vocabulary in the talk of adults and preschoolers during shared reading. *Journal of Early Childhood Research*, 4 (2), 153–167.

Uccelli, P., Demir-Lira, O. E., Rowe, M. L., Levine, S., & Goldin-Meakow, S. (2019). Children's early decontextualized talk predicts academic language proficiency in mid-adolescence. *Child Development*, 90(5), 1650–1663.

Van Kleeck, A., Alexander, E. I., Vigil, A., & Tempeton, K. E. (1996). Verbally modelling thinking for infants: Middle-class mothers' presentation of information structures during book sharing. *Journal of Research in Childhood Education*, 10(2), 101–113. doi:10.1080/02568549609594893.

Williams, G. (1999). The pedagogic device and the production of pedagogic discourse: A case study in early literacy education. In F. Christie (Ed.), *Pedagogy and the shaping of consciousness: Linguistic and social processes* (pp. 88–122). Cassell Academic.

Williams, G. (2001). Literacy pedagogy prior to schooling: Relations between social positioning and semantic variation. In A. Morais, I. Neves, B. Davies, & H. Baillie (Eds.), *Towards a sociology of pedagogy: The contribution of Basil Bernstein to research* (pp. 17–45). New York.

Zolotow, C., & Bobri, V. (1958). *Sleepy book*. Lothrop, Lee & Shepherd Co.

4   Shared Reading from Birth to Eighteen Months

Semiotic Beginnings

There is an inextricable connection between learning language, learning through language and learning about language (Halliday, 1993, 2003 [1980]). Lullabies, nursery rhymes and turn-taking games have distinctive linguistic patterns which draw infants' attention to the phonetic qualities of speech. The stylistic features of these literary forms, including repetition, alliteration and onomatopoeia, delight infants and encourage them to participate with others by moving their bodies to the rhythm and vocalising in unison with parents and siblings.

Before Birth

Studies of prenatal learning reveal that infants are born already familiar with the prosodic patterns of human speech, as they have been listening to the rhythms and cadences of their mother's voice for at least three months before they are born (Hepper & Shahidullah, 1994). Newborn infants prefer to listen to their mother's voice over the voices of other women (Cooper & Aslin, 1990; DeCasper & Fifer, 1980). They can detect subtle differences between speech sounds (phonemes); for example, they can distinguish between phonemes that are identical in place and manner of articulation, but differ in voicing, such as the phonemes /p/ and /b/ (Eimas et al., 1971).

It also appears that infants can learn while in the womb. DeCasper and Spence (1986) investigated whether infants who were exposed to particular speech patterns prior to birth would, after birth, prefer to listen to the same patterns rather than ones they had not heard before. Sixteen pregnant women read the first 28 paragraphs of *The Cat in the Hat* (Dr Seuss, 1957) aloud twice a day for the last six weeks of their pregnancy. After birth, each infant listened to a tape-recording of their mother's voice reading the text they had heard in the womb, and also a different but similar text they had not heard previously, *The King, the Mice and the Cheese* (Gurney and Gurney, 1965). The infants' responses were measured according to the frequency and strength with which they sucked on a pacifier. The infants all showed a preference for the text they had heard many times in the womb. DeCasper and Spence explained that

DOI: 10.4324/9781003168812-4

the foetuses had learned and remembered something about the acoustic cues ... e.g., prosodic cues such as syllabic beat, the voice-onset-time of consonants, the harmonic structure of sustained vowel sounds, and/or the temporal order of these sounds.

(DeCasper & Spence, 1986, p. 143)

The unique voice of the mother thus provides a strong connection to her child both before birth and after birth.

Each human voice expresses meanings and emotions through variations in pitch, intonation and loudness. The target texts chosen by DeCasper and Spence (1986) (*The Cat in the Hat* and *The King, the Mice and the Cheese*) were kept as similar as possible in terms of length and number of words, while differing in their acoustic qualities. From a functional linguistic perspective, the texts are examples of different registers. *The Cat in the Hat* is a type of humorous narrative poem that foregrounds the repetition of literary elements such as rhyme, alliteration, and a regular beat. In these respects it closely resembles the linguistic patterning of nursery rhymes. *The King, the Mice and the Cheese*, on the other hand, is an example of a narrative prose (story) register. Narratives typically focus on one or more individual characters who confront a problem that is resolved at the end. It is possible that the infants in DeCasper and Spence's (1986) study preferred to listen to the narrative poem read aloud because it was more distinctive acoustically compared with the narrative prose text, which (when read aloud) more closely resembled the patterns of everyday speech.

A Mother's Speech to her Child

Mothers play a critical but often invisible and unrecognised role in building the foundations of their child's future language and literacy development from the beginning of life. They do so by addressing their infant using two different but closely related registers; (1) infant-addressed speech, and (2) oral literature including nursery rhymes and lullabies. Both registers provide infants with rich and complementary experiences with language.

Infant-Addressed Speech

The term *infant-addressed speech* (also sometimes referred to as *motherese*) refers to the distinctive manner in which mothers and other caregivers speak to infants. Compared with the speech addressed to adults, infant-addressed speech has higher pitch and exaggerated intonation (Fernald, 1985), shorter utterances (Fernald, 1989), increased repetition (Fernald & Simon, 1984), and simplified grammar and a higher proportion of questions (Soderstrom et al., 2008). In addition, mothers extend the length of their vowel sounds when talking to infants, which has the effect of increasing the clarity of their speech by making the consonants stand out from the surrounding speech sounds (Burnham et al.,

2002). It has been suggested that infants prefer listening to infant-addressed speech because of this increased clarity (Liu et al., 2003).

Equally importantly, mothers' speech to infants carries a warm and affectionate cadence and is coupled with positive facial expressions (Soderstrom, 2007; Tamis-LeMonda et al., 2014). Gratier and Devouche (2017) capture the multimodal qualities of mothers' interactions with their infant in the following way; "When interacting with their mothers, newborns experience their faces moving in synchrony with the changing qualities of their voices, and they experience tactile stimulation, warmth, odours, and taste from the milk the mother provides" (p. 57). Neurologists have found that when an infant listens to infant-addressed speech, the infant's brain responds with increasing blood flow to the frontal cerebral area (Saito et al., 2007). Zangl and Mills (2007) also found that the brains of infants aged from 6 months to 13 months show increased neural activity when they listen to infant-addressed speech compared with adult-addressed speech.

Infants are active participants during interactions with their mothers (Golinkoff et al., 2015). Infants actively engage with their mothers during face to face interactions, which Trevarthen and Delafield-Butt (2016) refer to as "primary intersubjectivity", because the infant's sense of self, their subjectivity, depends on their engagement with another person (typically the mother), hence it is *inter*-personal, between persons. Such interactions play a vital role in building the foundations of language: "back-and-forth conversations that are both temporally and topically contingent on children's contribution, are the fuel that prime the learning of language" (Golinkoff et al., 2019, p. 988). Mothers weave their own talk around their infant's squeaks, gurgles, hiccups, sneezes, and other sounds, by commenting, asking questions, and then responding on behalf of the infant. Infants respond to their mother's initiations by imitating her facial expressions and vocalising (Gratier & Devouche, 2017).

A pattern of turn-taking is embedded in all aspects of daily life for an infant (Tamis-LeMonda et al., 2014). The release of mother's milk during breast-feeding involves a finely attuned interaction whereby a mother will gently "jiggle" the infant when necessary to keep her flow of milk coming (Kaye & Wells, 1980), thus the very process of receiving life-sustaining milk co-occurs with the to-and-fro patterning that underpins all human interaction. Furthermore, the act of suckling assists infants to develop the necessary musculature in their tongue, lips and larynx that will enable them to articulate speech sounds in the future. As Eliot (1999) points out, babbling includes some consonant sounds, particularly *b, d, m, n, w,* and *j*, and these sounds use the same muscles that are needed for sucking. Thus there is an inextricable connection between a mother's provision of nutrition and her infant's language development.

Caregiving routines such as bathing and nappy change all involve a predictable sequence of events, during which each participant, mother and baby, plays a role. Nappy change, for example, occurs several times a day, thus providing a regular opportunity for face-to-face interactions between mother and child. The infant gradually becomes accustomed to the sequence of events involved in the nappy change routine. The regularity and predictability of the routine allows the infant to focus more fully on her mother's face, mouth, lips and the sounds she is making. As infants begin to gain increasing control over the muscles of their vocal tract from around two months of age, they begin to make vowel-like, cooing sounds. These open sounds require less muscular control compared with consonantal sounds. Over the following months, infants engage in babbling (*bababab*a), which assists in the development of the vocal tract and enables the infant to experiment with sounds simply for the pleasure it affords them.

Nursery Rhymes and Lullabies

Parents in all cultures sing to their infants, either to settle them to sleep with lullabies, or to play with them and divert them with turn-taking games and songs (Trehub, 2017; Trehub, Unyk & Trainor, 1993). Nursery rhymes, lullabies and turn-taking games share some of the linguistic features of infant-addressed speech, such as repetition, shorter sentences and simplified grammar. Infants' earliest literary experiences involve the musical patterns of literary language spoken in the familiar voice of the mother, and the physical sensation of being rocked, patted and bounced. Even though infants cannot yet recognise the meanings of the words, the prosodic patterning and musicality of these small rhymes make them stand out from everyday talk during other familiar experiences such as feeding, nappy change and bath-time.

As they become increasingly adept at cooing and babbling, infants are able to participate in the recitation of nursery rhymes by vocalising in unison with parents, siblings and caregivers, regardless of whether they can produce or comprehend the spoken words of the rhyme. For example, Torr (1997) recorded her nine month old daughter loudly chanting /baba baba/ with her sister as she sang the nursery rhyme "baa baa black sheep". Halliday (1975) pointed out that one of the first "acts of meaning" he observed in his infant son Nigel served an imaginative function by creating "a world initially of pure sound" (p. 20).

A child's knowledge of nursery rhymes prior to school age is associated with their phonological awareness, which in turn is associated with future reading ability (Bryant et al., 1989; Bryant et al., 1990), even after the family's social background is taken into account. There are several factors that contribute to the potential of nursery rhymes to facilitate future language and literacy development. Like other forms of literature that have been transmitted orally across many generations, nursery rhymes contain words consisting of simple consonant-vowel syllables, and stylistic features such as rhyme, alliteration, and assonance, that render them easier to recognise and remember compared with everyday speech.

Nursery rhymes and turn-taking games also contribute to language development by providing infants with experience of the prosodic patterns of question and response during face-to-face conversational exchanges. Many nursery rhymes provide both sides of a conversation, and because they are regularly recited to infants during playful encounters, the linguistic and intonational patterning of questions and responses become familiar to them. Examples of two well-known nursery rhymes that contain features of dialogue are presented in Examples 4.1 and 4.2.

Example 4.1

> Simple Simon met a Pieman going to the fair. Said Simple Simon to the Pieman "let me taste your wares". Said the Pieman to Simple Simon "show me first your penny". Said Simple Simon to the Pieman "indeed I have not any".

Example 4.2

> Little boy blue come blow your horn. The sheep's in the meadow, the cow's in the corn. Where is the boy who looks after the sheep? He's under a haystack fast asleep. Will you wake him? No not I. For if I do, he's sure to cry.

Nursery rhymes provide infants with their first encounters with the narrative register. The well-known rhyme *Jack and Jill* is a highly condensed narrative, with an *orientation* (*Jack and Jill went up the hill to fetch a pail of water*), a *crisis* (*Jack fell down and broke his crown Jill came tumbling after*) and a *resolution* (*up Jack got and home did trot as fast as he could caper. He went to bed to mend his head with vinegar and brown paper*). Routine turn-taking games such as *This little piggy* and *Round and round the garden* follow a pattern of anticipation, suspense and resolution (Bruner, 1978), that also foreshadow some of the basic elements of narrative structure.

The linguistic patterning of nursery rhymes draws young children's attention to language structures and functions, while also providing opportunities for them to develop their aesthetic appreciation of verbal art. Such literary language is easily remembered and invites infants to chime in with familiar refrains, and respond physically by moving to the beat. Finger plays and rhymes often accompany the recitation of nursery rhymes, providing additional opportunities for verbal and motor development.

Reading Picture Books with Infants from Birth to Twelve Months

So far the discussion has focused on the importance of traditional oral literature for infants' early language and literacy development. Picture books tend to play a lesser role during this early stage of life, and there are few detailed studies of mothers reading picture books with their infant aged under 12 months. Yet many parents do begin to read to their infant in their first year (Karrass & Braungart-Rieker, 2005; Lamme & Packer, 1986) and research shows that infants who are read to at an early age have stronger language skills than those whose experience of reading begins at a later stage (DeBaryshe, 1993). Lamme and Packer (1986) provide one of the few detailed observational studies of mothers reading picture books with their infant. They videorecorded 13 mothers every week for four months, as each mother read four picture books aloud to her infant. The infants ranged in age from three to eight and a half months at the beginning of the study. Lamme and Packer (1986) identified the following stages through which infants pass during their first year of shared reading.

They found that for the first three months of life, infants engage in *receptive book-reading*. This phase involves very brief book-focused episodes (about three minutes), during which infants respond to shared reading by listening to their mother's voice while gazing at a picture, before becoming unsettled and turning away (Lamme & Packer, 1986). According to Fantz (1963), newborns prefer to look at black and white patterned surfaces rather than coloured surfaces, a finding that may be related to the fact that newborns initially have very limited visual acuity (Eliot, 1999). Zemac and Teller (2007) found that twelve week old infants prefer coloured stimuli over white stimuli. In his study of 20 infants ranging in age from 3 days to 3 months of age, Adams (1987) found that infants preferred the colour red most of all, followed by yellow and blue. Green was the infants' least preferred colour. This colour preference confirmed the findings of Bornstein (1975). It has also been demonstrated that infants prefer to look at pictures of human faces instead of patterns (Duuren et al., 2009; Fantz, 1963).

The next phase identified by Lamme and Packer (1986), from three to six months of age, is *random book awareness*. They found that mothers would notice what their child was looking at in an illustration, point to it and name it. Infants sometimes touched or patted their mother's arm as she read to them. Hardman and Jones (1999) described how infants at this age interacted physically with a book in the same way they would with other objects, by grabbing, handling, patting, scratching and sucking it. Eliot (1999) explains that, by six months, infants' vision has become highly developed: "By 6 months of age all her primary visual abilities will have emerged, such as depth perception, color vision, fine acuity, and well-controlled eye movements" (p. 196).

Lamme and Packer (1986) identified behaviours from six to nine months that they referred to as *considered book involvement*. During this phase, infants become actively engaged in book reading, by vocalising, pointing, touching and grabbing the picture book. They may attempt to turn the pages, and have increased understanding of the rituals and practices involved in the activity of shared reading. The next phase, from 9 to 12 months, is referred to by Lamme and Packer (1986) as *active book reading*. Infants can now orient a book correctly, right way up, and turn the pages. By 12 months, infants have full vision (Eliot, 1999). They actively participate during the reading by making animal noises and the sounds of car engines and sirens, and may begin to identify familiar objects depicted in pictures by pointing and/or attempting to name them.

Lamme and Packer (1986) refer to the stage from 12 to 15 months as *joint book reading*. Infants now play an active role by pointing to the pictures and naming familiar objects. Infants can now understand some words and join in with familiar rhymes and refrains (I'll huff and I'll puff and blow your house down). They point to pictures and ask for a name (what's that?). They engage in a type of pretend play by kissing a picture of a character who fell over, or pretend to "eat" a piece of birthday cake represented in a picture, or drink a cup of tea poured by Polly who put the kettle on. The 10 to 14 month old infants in Penfold and Bacharach's (1988) study spent more time looking at the pictures in highly illustrated picture books compared with time spent looking at minimally illustrated picture books.

The Protolanguage

Semiotic Beginnings

The ability of infants to identify some familiar objects in picture books corresponds with their ability to communicate with familiar others by using sound symbolically to express meaning, in a phase of development that Halliday (1975) refers to as the protolanguage.

Towards the end of their first year, infants begin to produce their first "acts of meaning" by combining a sound or gesture consistently to express a particular meaning. Such expression-content utterances are referred to by Halliday (1975) as *signs*. For example, one 11 month old child produced /mama/ as a generalised request form to obtain food items that she could see on the table in front of her. The same child used the sign /aluh aluh/ as an expression of affection and closeness with family members (Torr, 1986, 2015).

Halliday (1975) posited that infants' signs are inherently different from their other forms of communicating (vocalising, crying, cooing, and babbling). Rather, they resemble the adult language in having a content and an expression, but unlike in the adult language, they cannot combine words together to form grammatical structures. The meaning of a sign is unlike the meaning of a word in the adult language, as the meaning of a sign is broad, generalised and often idiosyncratic; for example "let's look at this together", "I want one of the bread rolls I can see on the table". Since they do not resemble adult words, signs are often interpretable only by close family members in the here-and-now moment in which they are uttered. In order for parents, educators and others to interact effectively with infants during the protolanguage, they must "learn" their infant's protolanguage.

The Microfunctions

Halliday (1975) carefully observed the development of his infant son Nigel to determine the functions (referred to as microfunctions) served by the signs of the protolanguage.

- The Instrumental microfunction "is the function that language serves of satisfying the child's material needs, of enabling him to obtain the goods and services he wants" (ibid., p. 19). Nigel used these signs to obtain food, toys and other desired objects that were visible to him at the time of utterance.
- The Regulatory microfunction "is the function of language as controlling the behavior of others" (ibid., p. 19). The focus of regulatory signs is to direct the behaviours of others; for example, to sing a song or play a game with the infant.
- The Interactional microfunction "is the language used by the child to interact with those around him, particularly his mother and others that are important to him" (ibid., p. 19). Nigel used these signs to establish, express and maintain closeness with another; for example, through greetings and shared attention to pictures: "the utterance directs attention to a particular object, typically a picture, which is then used as the channel for interacting with this other person" (ibid., p. 23).
- The Personal microfunction "is language used to express the child's own uniqueness" (ibid., p. 20). Nigel used these signs to express his feelings and responses to aspects of his environment.
- The Imaginative microfunction "is the function whereby the child creates an environment of his own" (ibid., p. 20). These signs were produced during pretend play, for example pretending to be a lion by roaring, or making an engine noise while playing with a toy train.

The signs of the protolanguage are systematic in the sense that the child uses them consistently over weeks or months to express a similar cluster of meanings. They are functional, as they can be interpreted as serving a particular purpose in the child's life. And they show continuity with the adult system because the purposes they serve are an early manifestation of the highly abstract metafunctions that organise the words and structures of the adult language; the experiential, interpersonal and textual metafunctions served by language.

The microfunctions can be seen as foreshadowing the functional organisation of the adult system as they enable infants to use their signs to act on the world by controlling the behaviour of their partner (the regulatory function) or by requesting desired foods or objects from them (the instrumental function). Alternatively infants may use their microfunctional signs to express warmth and affection for their conversational partner (interactional function) or to express their feelings in response to the world around them (personal function). The infant's conversational partners respond to commands and requests by either providing the desired objects or services, or by refusing to do so. In either case, the infant's act of meaning will have been interpreted and responded to, thus enhancing the child's confidence in their semiotic capability. These microfunctional contexts are represented in Table 4.1.

While Table 4.1 presents a clear distinction between language for acting on the world (regulatory and instrumental functions) and language for reflecting on the world (interactional and personal functions), it is less clear where to locate the imaginative microfunction served by language within this framework.

Table 4.1 Functional organisation of microfunctions

	Person	Object
Action	Regulatory microfunction	Instrumental microfunction
Reflection	Interactional microfunction	Personal microfunction

Shared Reading and the Imaginative Function

The functioning of the imagination exists on a different plane from the satis-faction of physical wants and needs (instrumental and regulatory signs) and the quest for love and human connection (interactional and personal signs). Ima-gination is defined as "mental faculty forming images of external objects not present to the senses" (Oxford University Press, 1964, p. 604). Imagination is associated with qualities such as creativity, fantasy, make believe, invention, and other intangibles. The imaginative microfunction of the protolanguage is the earliest manifestation of what will eventually evolve into the mature aesthetic appreciation of literature in its many forms.

There is a clear connection here between the shared reading of picture books and the development of the imaginative function of language. Shared reading is associated with future success in learning to read, thus playing a central role in the development of academic knowledge. Literary texts such as poetry and imagina-tive writing are entirely constituted through language, and infants who are read to from birth have multiple opportunities to become familiar with and enjoy this type of interaction. Shared reading cannot occur without the input, gui-dance and support of a mediating adult, typically the child's mother, and other adults within the child's family circle. As Hasan (2006) notes, "the dominant focus of research [on language development] has remained on what the chil-dren said when, where and how, rather than on the significance of the sayings of the adults with whom the children interact" (p. 159).

The importance of the imaginative function for future language and literacy development cannot be overstated. Torr's (1986, 1987, 1997) longitudinal case study of her daughter Annie's protolanguage revealed that Annie's use of signs to serve an interactional function were almost always produced while looking at pictures in books or singing songs, thus suggesting that she saw interactional, personal and imaginative microfunctions as serving the same broader function.

Two closely related activities provide the context for the early development of the imaginative function in the protolanguage: pretend play and shared reading. Pretend play involves the imaginative reconstruction of some aspect of experience. The earliest forms of pretend play occurred during the protolanguage, for example a child says "*shhh*" while putting teddy to bed, or makes "clicking" sounds when feeding her doll, or engine noises while pushing her toy car. The incorporation of the infant's signs into the role play situation shows a gradual freeing of the sign from its original context of use. The analysis of infants' imaginative signs reveals infants' emerging awareness that the linguistic system can be manipulated in the recreation of personally salient experiences.

Annie's first clear act of pretence occurred at 10 and a half months, and like almost all her imaginative uses of language it involved picture books either directly or indirectly. Please see Example 4.3.

Example 4.3

> Clara aged 30 months old was sitting on her bed listening to her mother reading a picture book. Younger sister Annie (10.5 months) was playing on the floor. She deliberately pulled herself up on Clara's bed, rested her head on Clara's pillow, closed her eyes and made soft cooing sounds. She then opened her eyes and smiled broadly, as if to indicate that she was pretending.

Unlike pretend play, shared reading involves an active, sustained focus on a semiotic artefact, a picture book. Infants must engage in an act of imagination for shared reading to be meaningful.

Shared Reading, Aesthetic Appreciation, and Favourite Books

Shared reading provides infants with an experience of visual and verbal art. While there are many commonalities in infants' responses to the world around them, they also begin to show preferences for some aspects of their environment over others, suggesting that the genesis of aesthetic awareness occurs early in life. Danko-McGhee explains:

> when they [infants] see something that they like (a preference), and they respond to it through the senses by wanting to touch the viewed object or image, fixate upon it, smile at it, or use any other body language to convey that they like it, then this is an aesthetic response.
>
> (Danko-McGhee, 2010, pp. 356–367)

In her analysis of the linguistic features of nursery rhymes, Hasan (1985) draws attention to the fact that nursery rhymes not only facilitate children's early language learning, but also, and equally importantly, they facilitate their aesthetic appreciation of verbal art. Infants respond to the musicality of lyrical texts with their whole bodies, moving their limbs, smiling and laughing. Initially they gain pleasure simply in making noise in unison with another child. The sounds of music and singing are particularly pleasurable to infants. Torr (1997) notes that Annie devoted considerable effort to joining in with her mother and sister in the performance of rhymes and songs. She also attempted to imitate her older sister by producing stylised finger movements to the rhyme "Twinkle Twinkle Little Star".

Shared reading provides infants with an opportunity to have aesthetic experiences which engage and move them in intangible ways. Most infants have one or more favourite picture books which they wish to share over and over again. Straub (2009) suggests that young children's favourite picture books provide them with experiences that affect them deeply. Kiefer (1988) explains that, when young children have the opportunity to respond deeply to picture books, it may "lead children to develop a lifelong interest in books and a lifetime appreciation of art" (p. 12).

Shared Reading with an Infant during the Protolanguage: A Snapshot

Example 4.4

> [*Alex, 16 months, is playing with his toys on the floor. He picks up one of his picture books,* Moo, Baa, La La La *(Boynton, 2011 [1984]) and attempts to climb onto his father Ben's lap. The book contains line drawings of cows, pigs, sheep, dogs, cats, ducks and horses, all drawn in a simple cartoon style against a plain background.*]

BEN: [*settling Alex comfortably on his lap*] Hey buddy. Want to read a book?
ALEX: [*patting the book*] Book. Book.
BEN: [*pointing to the picture of a cow*] What does a cow say?
ALEX: Mooooo. Mooooo.
BEN: [*pointing at the second page*] What does a sheep say?
ALEX: Baa baa baa
BEN: [*reading the printed text on the third page*] Three singing pigs say …?
ALEX: *Lalalala.*
BEN: [*reading the fourth page*] "No no" you say "that isn't right. The pigs say …?
ALEX: [*makes snuffling noises, touching his nose*].
BEN: [*laughs*] That's right! [*pointing at a picture of a rhinoceroses, Ben pauses*] What do rhinoceroses say?
ALEX: [*produces more snuffling noises, then grabs the book and turns the page to reveal a pictures of cats. He makes a squeaking noise while jabbing the page with his finger*]
BEN: Uh oh, what's happening to the kittens?
ALEX: That! That!
BEN: That's right. [*pointing*] Uh oh. The big dogs are chasing the kittens. Oh no, do you think the kittens will get away from the big dogs? Let's see what happens. [*Alex grabs the book again. He skips a page and now they are on the last page*]
BEN: [*reads*] Shhhhh! [*holding a finger to his lips, he reads in a whisper*] It's quiet now. [*he points at Alex*] What do **you** say?
ALEX: [*laughs, points at Ben, and makes different animal sounds*]. Moo. Baa. Moo. Baa.
BEN: [*laughing and tickling Alex*] I say I love you!

This brief interaction, part game and part picture book sharing, shows how the simplest of book-focused experiences is rich in opportunities for learning. Ben responds readily to Alex's invitation to read, showing his son that he values books and reading. Ben verbally refers to Alex as a reader (*want to read a book?*) as he helps Alex clamber onto his lap in a welcoming embrace. Alex and his father jointly contribute to the meaning-making, each according to his own capabilities. Ben uses his voice and gestures in an expressive way to encourage Alex's participation. Ben's questions and comments guide Alex into ways of making meaning from picture books, such as prediction (*Do you think the kittens will get away from the big dogs? Let's see what happens*).

Alex, who is still in the early stages of the protolanguage phase, already knows many things about reading. He knows that books are entertaining, they are handled in certain ways, pictures convey meaning, and those meanings can be talked about. No-one has ever explicitly taught Alex these facts. He has learnt them through frequent experiences of being read to by his parents and caregivers. Doonan (1993) explains the importance of providing infants with the opportunity to have a personal response to literature: "By playing with the ideas provoked by a work of art, we create something of our own from it" (p. 7). The qualities of the text contribute to the language learning opportunities presented by shared reading. The rhyme and rhythm of the text resonate with the patterns of nursery rhymes and other forms of oral literature.

Such patterned language facilitates Alex's awareness that the literary language in picture books differs from everyday speech. Rhyme also facilitates the ability to remember the lines. The last page of the book disrupts the regular pattern of statements about the sounds made by various animals by directly addressing the child reader (*what do you say?*). Alex is familiar with this ending and anticipates it eagerly. He enjoys making up nonsense answers to this final question on the last page. With the gentle guidance and encouragement of his father, Alex is able to achieve through interaction with a more knowledgeable reader and viewer what he could not yet achieve on his own.

It is through these linguistic and illustrative games that a tension is created between reality and its literary re-creation, demonstrating that words have meaning and force beyond their literal meanings. Language play in picture books assists children to understand and appreciate literary metaphor, where a similarity is drawn between entities which would not normally be seen as alike. Metaphor is a vehicle for abstract thinking which is necessary for accessing different academic disciplines.

Concluding Remarks

This chapter traces the developmental trajectories of infants' language development from before birth to around 18 months of age. From birth, nursery rhymes and lullabies provide infants with early experiences of "verbal art". During the protolanguage, infants engage in acts of meaning using their own invented expressions to serve a range of functions. One function, the imaginative function, is especially significant for many reasons. Shared reading of picture books serves a unique purpose in supporting children's emotional and aesthetic development. The first two years of life are crucial for infants' development across all domains, and literary texts and shared reading of picture books provide a language rich introduction to the pleasures afforded by books and reading.

References

Adams, R. J. (1987). An evaluation of color preference in early infancy. *Infant Behavior and Development*, 10, 143–150.

Bornstein, M. H. (1975). Qualities of color vision in infancy. *Journal of Experimental Psychology*, 19(3), 401–419. doi:10.1016/0022-0965(75)90070-90073.

Boynton, S. (2011 [1984]). *Moo, baa, la la la!* Little Simon.

Bruner, J. S. (1978). "The role of dialogue in language acquisition". In A. Sinclair, R. J. Jarvella, & W. J. M. Levelt (Eds.), *The child's conception of language* (pp. 241–256). Springer.

Bryant, P. E., Bradley, L., MacLean, M., & Crossland, J. (1989). Nursery rhymes, phonological skills and reading. *Journal of Child Language*, 16(2), 407–428. doi:10.1017/S0305000900010485.

Bryant, P. E., MacLean, P. E., Bradley, M., & Crossland, L. L. (1990). Rhyme and alliteration, phoneme detection, and learning to read. *Developmental Psychology*, 26(3), 429–438.

Burnham, D., Kitamura, C., & Vollmer-Conna, U. (2002). What's new, pussycat? On talking to babies and animals. *Science*, 269, 1435. www.jstor.org/stable3076750.

Oxford University Press. (1964). Imagination. In *Concise Oxford Dictionary*. Oxford University Press.

Cooper, R. P., & Aslin, R. N. (1990). Preference for infant-directed speech in the first month after birth. *Child Development* 61(5), 1584–1595. www.jtor.org/stable/1130766.

Danko-McGhee, K. (2010). The aesthetic preferences of infants: Pictures of faces that capture their interest. *Contemporary Issues in Early Childhood*, 11(4), 365–387. doi:10.2304/ciec.2010.11.4.365.

DeBaryshe, B. D. (1993). Joint picture-book reading correlates of early oral language skill. *Journal of Child Language*, 20, 455–461. doi:10.1017/S0305000900008370.

DeCasper, A. J. & Fifer, W. P. (1980). Of human bonding: Newborns prefer their mother's voices. *Science*, 208, 1174–1176.

DeCasper, A. J. & Spence, M. J. (1986) Prenatal material speech influences newborns' perception of speech sounds. *Infant Behavior and Development*, 9, 133–150.

Doonan, J. (1993). *Looking at pictures in picture books*. Thimble Press.

Dr Seuss (T. Geisel). (1957). *The cat in the hat*. Random House.

Duuren, M., Kendell-Scott, L. & Stark, N. (2009) Early aesthetic choices: Infant preferences for attractive premature infant faces, *Advances in Psychological Science*, 17(6), 1234–1241.

Eimas, P. D., Siqueland, E. R., Jusczyk, P., & Vigorito, J. (1971). Speech perception in infants. *Science*, 171(3968), 303–306. doi:10.1126/science.171.3968.303.

Eliot, L. (1999). *Early intelligence: How the mind and brain develop in the first five years*. Penguin.

Fantz, R. L. (1963), Pattern vision in newborn infants. *Science*, 140(3564), 296–297.

Fernald, A. (1985). Four-month-old infants prefer to listen to motherese. *Infant Behavior and Development*, 8, 181–195. doi:1016/s0163-6383(85080005-9).

Fernald, A. (1989). Intonation and communicative intent in mothers' speech to infants: Is the melody the message? *Child Development*, 60, 1497–1510. doi:10.2307/1130938.

Fernald, A., & Simon, T. (1984). Expanded intonation contours in mothers' speech to newborns. *Developmental Psychology*, 20, 104–113.

Golinkoff, R. M., Can, D. D., Soderstrom, M., & Hirsh-Pasek, K. (2015). (Baby) talk to me: The social context of infant-directed speech and its effects on early language acquisition. *Current Directions in Psychological Science*, 24(5), 339–344. www.jstor.org/stable/44318893.

Golinkoff, R. M., Hoff, E., Rowe, M. L., Tamis-LeMonda, C. S., & Hirsh-Pasek, K. (2019). Language matters: Denying the existence of the 30-million-word gap has serious consequences. *Child Development*, 90(3), 985–992. doi:10.11/cdev.13128.

Gratier, M., & Devouche, E. (2017). The development of infant participation in communication. In M. Filippa, P. Kuhn & B. Westrup (Eds.), *Early vocal contact and pre-term infant brain development* (pp. 55–68). Springer.

Gurney, N., & Gurney, E. (1965). *The King, the Mice and the Cheese*. Beginner Books.

Halliday, M. A. K. (1975). *Learning how to mean: Explorations in the development of language*. Edward Arnold.

Halliday, M. A. K. (1993). Towards a language-based theory of learning. *Linguistics and Education*, 5, 93–116.

Halliday, M. A. K. (2003 [1980]). Three aspects of children's language development: Learning language, learning through language, learning about language. In J. J. Webster (Ed.), *The collected works of M. A. K. Halliday* (The language of early childhood, Volume 4) (pp. 308–326). Bloomsbury Academic.

Hardman, M., & Jones, L. (1999). Sharing books with babies: An evaluation of an early literacy intervention. *Educational Review*, 51(3) 221–229. doi:10.1080/00131919997461.

Hasan, R. (1985). *Linguistics, language and verbal art*. Deakin University Press.

Hasan, R. (2006). The world in words: Semiotic mediation, tenor and ideology. In G. Williams & A. Lukin (Eds.), *Development of language: Functional perspectives on species and individuals* (pp. 158–181). Bloomsbury Publishing.

Hepper, P. G., & Shahidullah, B. S. (1994). Development of fetal hearing. *Archives of Disease in Childhood*, 71, 81–87.

Hoff, E. (2006). How social contexts support and shape language development. *Developmental Review*, 26(1), 55–88.

Karrass, J., & Braungart-Rieker, J. M. (2005). Effects of shared parent-infant book reading on early language acquisition. *Applied Developmental Psychology*, 26, 133–148. doi:10.1016/j.appdev.2004.12.003.

Kaye, K., & Wells, A. J. (1980). Mothers' jiggling and the burst-pause pattern in neonatal feeding. *Infant Behavior and Development*, 3, 29–46. doi:10.1016S0163(80)80005–80001.

Kiefer, B. (1988). Picture books as contexts for literary, aesthetic, and real world understandings. *Language Arts*, 65(3), 260–271.

Liu, H. M., Kuhl, P. K., & Tsao, F. M. (2003). An association between mothers' speech clarity and infants' speech discrimination skills. *Developmental Science*, 6, F1–F10.

Lamme, L. L., & Packer, A. B. (1986). Bookreading behaviors of infants. *The Reading Teacher*, 39(6), 504–509. www.jstor.org/stable/20199147.

Painter, C. (1984). *Into the mother tongue*. Frances & Pinter.

Penfold, K., & Bacharach, V. R. (1988). Reading to young children: The impact of illustrations in children's books. *International Journal of Early Childhood*, 20(35).

Saito, Y., Aoyama, S., Kondo, T., Fukumoto, R., Konishi, N., Nakamura, K., Kobayashi, M., & Toshima, T. (2007). Frontal cerebral blood flow change associated with infant- directed speech. *Archives of Disease in Childhood: Fetal and Neonatal Edition*, 92, F113–F116. doi:10.1136/adc.2006.097949.

Soderstrom, M. (2007). Beyond babytalk: Re-evaluating the nature and content of speech input to preverbal infants. *Developmental Review*, 27(4), 501–532. doi:10.1016/j.dr.2007.06.002.

Soderstrom, M., Blossom, M., Foygal, R., & Morgan, J. L. (2008). Acoustical cues and grammatical units in speech to two preverbal infants. *Journal of Child Language*, 35(4), 869–902. doi:1017/S0305000908008763.

Straub, S. (2009). The power of reading with babies. *Infant Observation*, 12(3), 349–352. doi:10.1080/13698030903303706.

Tamis-LeMonda, C. S., Kuchirko, Y., & Song, L. (2014). Why is infant language learning faciliated by parental responsiveness? *Current Directions in Psychological Science* 23(2), 121–126. doi:10.1177/0963721414522813.

Torr, J. (published as Oldenburg). (1986). The transitional stage of a second child – 18 months to 2 years. *Australian Review of Applied Linguistics*, 9(1), 123–135.

Torr, J. (published as Oldenburg). (1987). Learning the language and learning through language in early childhood. In M. A. K. Halliday, J. Gibbons, & H. Nicholas (Eds.), *Learning, keeping and using language* (pp. 27–38). John Benjamins.

Torr, J. (1997). *From child tongue to mother tongue: A case study of language development in the first two and a half years.* Monographs in Systemic Linguistics, 9. University of Nottingham.

Torr, J. (2015). Language development in early childhood: Learning how to mean. In J. J. Webster (Ed.), *The Bloomsbury companion to M. A. K. Halliday* (pp. 242–256). Bloomsbury.

Trehub, S. E. (2017). The maternal voice as a special signal for infants. In M. Filippa, P. Kuhn & B. Westrup (Eds.), *Early vocal contact and pre-term infant brain development* (pp. 39–54). Springer.

Trehub, S. E., Unyk, A. M., & Trainor, L. J. (1993). Adults identify infant-directed music across cultures. *Infant behavior and Development*, 16(2), 193–211.

Trevarthen, C., & Delafield-Butt, J. (2016). Intersubjectivity and the imagination and feelings of the infant: Implications for education in the early years. Under-three year olds in policy and practice. In E White & C. Dalli (Eds.), *Under-three year olds in policy and practice. Policy and pedagogy with under-three year olds: Cross-disciplinary insights and innovations* (pp. 17–40). Springer. doi:10.1007/978-981-10-2275-3_2.

Zangl, R., & Mills, D. L. (2007). Increased brain activity to infant-addressed speech in 6- and 13-month-old infants. *Infancy*, 11(1), 31–62.

Zemach, I. K., & Teller, D. Y. (2007). Infant color vision: Infants' spontaneous color preferences are well behaved. *Vision Research*, 47(10), 1362–1367. doi:10.1016/j.visres.2007.02.002.

5 Shared Reading from Eighteen to Twenty-Four Months
Representing Experience

In the second half of their second year, many children undergo a rapid increase in the number of words they produce and understand. Shared reading of picture books provides children with the opportunity to encounter many new and unusual words that they are unlikely to encounter in other contexts. The depth and breadth of a child's vocabulary serves as a proxy for their general knowledge about the world and is a predictor of their success in learning to read after they commence school. Although shared reading with this age group is usually brief, sometimes only a few minutes, it provides a language-rich context for meaning making. Shared reading not only facilitates language development but also provides a rich entrée into the world of books and reading. The more infants enjoy shared reading, the more motivated they will be to engage with books whenever they can. This chapter will describe language development from 18 to 24 months according to the tenets of systemic functional linguistic (SFL) theory (Halliday, 1975, 1994). SFL theory posits that language is shaped by the functions it serves in the lives of speakers. How shared reading supports infants' development of language as a resource for learning during this transitional period will be the central focus in this chapter.

Learning Language and Learning through Language: 18–24 months

Halliday (1975) referred to the linguistic developments that take place between 18 and 24 months as *transitional* in nature. In order to appreciate why this period of language development is considered transitional, according to SFL theory, it is necessary to provide a brief summary of the developmental achievements of the phase that precedes this transitional phase; that is, the protolanguage (Chapter 4). During the protolanguage, from about 10–18 months of age, infants communicate with a small circle of family members using a system of invented expressions ("signs") that convey broad and generalised meanings. These signs serve four distinct functions. On the one hand they enable the infant to request objects and direct the behaviour of a partner (instrumental and regulatory functions respectively) and on the other hand they enable infants to experience togetherness with others and express their personal feelings (interpersonal and personal functions respectively). A fifth function involves the expression of an imaginative function.

DOI: 10.4324/9781003168812-5

At some point around 18 months of age, infants begin to produce some recognisably adult words while decreasing their use of their own invented sign systems. This development enables infants to communicate more effectively with a wider circle of acquaintances in their speech community. As Gratier and Devouche explain:

> It is thus on the basis of established, often idiosyncratic, shared understanding that infants learn to reshape sounds and bodily expressions that are already meaningful (to the people most important to them) in order to render them accessible to a wider group of social partners.
>
> (Gratier & Devouche, 2017, p. 63)

During the period from 18–24 months, infants' utterances become less tied to the immediate material setting in which they are produced. This is evident when infants begin to use their new adult-like words to refer to objects that are not in their field of vision. For example, 20 month old Annie pointed to the empty shelf in her bedroom where her teddy usually sat, and said *teddy*. It was clear from her tone that she was not requesting the teddy, but rather using her language to comment on its absence. Not long afterwards, on a trip to visit her grandparents, Annie repeated the word *dog* several times, in anticipation of playing with their pet on arrival. Children's emerging realisation that words can be used to refer to the past and predict the future paves the way for the development of naming as a vehicle for learning more generally.

The number of recognisable adult-like words produced and understood by infants increases exponentially during this period. Yet infants' newly learnt words and structures are not entirely free of contextual constraints in the way that adult words (lexis) are. Specifically, during this transitional phase, infants' words and structures undergo a process of functional reorganisation, such that they can now be used *either* to request objects and to direct the behaviour of another person (a *pragmatic function*), *or* to reflect on some aspect of the environment (a *mathetic function*) (Halliday, 1975). Halliday (1975) referred to these two functions served by language during this period as *macrofunctions*.

The children whose language has been analysed using systemic functional linguistic theory, Nigel (Halliday, 1975), Hal (Painter, 1984) and Annie (Torr, 1997), made this functional distinction between pragmatic and mathetic contexts explicit in two ways. First, they used one group of words exclusively in pragmatic contexts, to obtain goods and services, and another group of words exclusively in mathetic contexts, to comment on some aspect of their experience. For example, at 19.5 months of age, Annie used the words *apple, cheese, drink, juice, milk,* and *toast* to request these food items (*I want* …). Nevertheless, she never used these same words in more reflective contexts (*there's a* …), as for example when seeing these items depicted in her picture books. Similarly, another child Jay used the word "apple" to refer to an actual apple, red balloons and balls, and the red wooden sphere on top of a picket fence post. He never used the word "apple" to request the food item. In requesting contexts, he pointed at an apple and said "that, have that".

Secondly, the three children made the distinction between pragmatic and mathetic contexts explicit in their pronunciation. Nigel and Hal produced all their pragmatic utterances on a rising or level tone, while Annie produced hers with a tense voice quality. Mathetic utterances, on the other hand, were produced on a falling tone by Nigel and Hal, with a lax voice quality by Annie. Each child maintained this functional distinction between "language for doing" (Pragmatic) and "language for learning" (Mathetic) for several months during this transitional period of language growth. The protolinguistic signs of the preceding phase had been reorganised according to two more generalised and abstract functions. The instrumental and regulatory utterances of the protolanguage were now realised in a more generalised form, as demands for goods and services. The interactional, personal and imaginative utterances of the protolanguage evolved into a more generalised function served by language; that is, as a vehicle for learning, serving a mathetic ("learning") function in the children's lives.

Shared Reading and the Mathetic Macrofunction

Almost without exception, Annie's use of mathetic language (language for learning) during the period from 18 to 24 months occurred only during one-to-one shared reading of picture books with her mother (Torr, 1997). In other words, shared reading of picture books was for Annie the primary context in which she used her developing language as a vehicle for learning. According to Halliday (1975), the mathetic function of language is "the use of the symbolic system not as a means of acting on reality but as a means of learning about reality" (p. 106). Shared reading of picture books often serves as a springboard for extra-textual discussions during which many parents and educators offer additional information, explanations and definitions, above and beyond what is presented in the picture book text itself. Please see Examples 5.1 and 5.2.

Example 5.1

ANNIE: [*looking at a picture of a duck driving an old-fashioned car*] Who that? Doggie. Duck. Duck.
MOTHER: Mmm. That's a funny old car!
ANNIE: Go.
MOTHER: Yes. That's what they used to drive in the olden days, didn't they?
ANNIE: Go.
MOTHER: Going along is it?
ANNIE: Go, go, go.

Example 5.2

ANNIE: [*looking in book*] What's that?
MOTHER: Um, that's a rat. A rat is like a big mouse.

As children become more adept at using language to communicate, so too the adult's explanations become increasingly detailed and often include technical terminology and definitions that extend far beyond the content of the picture book itself.

Language and the Representation of Experience

Children's language growth during this transitional period comprised three main areas; naming, information exchange, and dialogue.

Naming

One of the most obvious indicators that children's language is changing during the latter half of the second year is the rapid increase in the number of adult-like words that a child knows and understands. Children learn new words through interactions with more knowledgeable speakers, and shared reading provides a particularly rich context for word learning because adults talk more to infants during shared reading than they do in any other context (Clemens & Kegel, 2021; Soderstrom & Wittebolle, 2013). Furthermore, shared reading provides additional support for word learning because the meanings of words are supported by the illustrations.

When parents and educators read picture books with children during this phase of development, they focus on naming and thus support infants' early vocabulary growth in "word consciousness" (Christ & Wang, 2010). Lee (2011) found that the number of words a child can produce at the age of two years predicts their language and literacy skills up to eight years later, even after controlling for socioeconomic status, gender, birth order and ethnicity. Example 5.3 is typical of the parent-infant book-focused interactions that occur early in the transitional phase.

Example 5.3

MOTHER: Where's the elephant? Can you see an elephant anywhere?
ANNIE: That? That?
MOTHER: There's an elephant there. You find him. Where's the elephant?
ANNIE: That.
MOTHER: Is that an elephant?
ANNIE: [*pointing at camel*] There. There. There.
MOTHER: No, that's a camel.
ANNIE: There.
MOTHER: And what's that one? Is that an elephant? That's a bear.
ANNIE: That. That.
MOTHER: Right. A flower.
ANNIE: That. That. That.
MOTHER: Rabbit.

ANNIE: Rabbit, rabbit, rabbit. There.
MOTHER: Lion.
ANNIE: There.
MOTHER: There's the lion in his bed. See the lion in his bed?
ANNIE: There.
MOTHER: And where's the moon?
ANNIE: Moon.
MOTHER: Moon, that's right.
ANNIE: Not there!
MOTHER: Have you had enough of this story? Do you want another one?
ANNIE: Yeah.

By 24 months, children play an active role during shared reading, using language to initiate interactions and to ask questions. Nevertheless, the meanings expressed in illustrations are not transparent and infants still need much support to recognise and name entities depicted in pictures, as can be seen in Example 5.4.

Example 5.4

MOTHER: [*asking 23 month old Annie which picture book she would like to read*]
    Shall we have this one called "busy teddy bear"?
ANNIE: No.
MOTHER: No. Don't want that one?
ANNIE: [*pointing at book*] That.
MOTHER: This one? [*reading*] "We help Daddy". There's a little girl and a little
    boy and a daddy, and they're all working in the garden.
ANNIE: [*pointing at the picture*] There.
MOTHER: There they are. The little children are having a ride on Daddy's
    wheelbarrow. Your daddy does that, doesn't he?
ANNIE: Yeah.
MOTHER: Mm.
ANNIE: There mum … mum.
MOTHER: That's right. The mummy.
ANNIE: [*pointing at picture of a little boy*] Daddy.
MOTHER: Is that the daddy? Or is that the little boy? I think that's a little boy.
    Let's see what else is in here. Can you see a puppy dog? [*continues looking at
    pictures*]

Adult support is important because much of the meaning in picture books for infants is expressed through the pictures. In *Wobble Pop* (Burningham, 1984), for example, each page contains one printed word representing a single observable material process (a "doing" verb); for example, knock, sweep, drip, scrub. The illustrations, however, are rich with information that elaborates on the meaning of the word in the context of the actions of two characters, a child and a teddy, as they go about cleaning a house. Mishaps include spilling a bucket of water and accidently bumping their heads together while trying swat a fly, neither of which are referred to in the printed text. The last page shows them wearily heading home after a busy day. Like many picture books for this age group, the story is recounted through the pictures, leaving scope for plentiful and interesting adult–child conversations.

Classification and Building Taxonomies

When children name objects depicted in picture books, they are making generalisations; for example, a child may use the word *duck* to refer to a bath toy, a picture of a duck wearing clothes in a picture book, and an actual duck in the river, despite the differences in colour, shape, size, and function. Educational knowledge categorises phenomena into classes according to various criteria. For examples, ducks, owls, swans, and storks are all classified under the category "birds". Shared reading of picture books provides a context in which parents and educators not only name entities but also classify them in various ways, as expressed in Example 5.5.

Example 5.5

MOTHER: Oh, they're little ducks, called ducklings.
ANNIE: [*stabbing at the page with her finger*] Duck, duck, duck, duck, duck, duck, duck.
MOTHER: What are they? Quack, quack.
ANNIE: Duck, duck, duck, duck.
MOTHER: Duck, yes, duck. Any other ducks?
ANNIE: Duck.
MOTHER: Yes, duck. And what are these?
ANNIE: Duck.
MOTHER: No, they look like ducks, but they're really swans. Can you say swan?
ANNIE: [*vocalising*]
MOTHER: And there are some other birds called owls. And they go "toowit toowoo".
ANNIE: [*imitates owl sound*]
MOTHER: Birdies.
ANNIE: [*indicates she now wants a different book*].

The pictures in this book provided the mother with an opportunity to explain that although some animals (ducks, swans, and owls) are all members of the class "bird" (*some birds are called owls*) and even look similar (*they look like ducks*), they are nevertheless categorised differently as reflected in the fact that they have different names. The mother's use of verbal processes creates a distinction between entities that exist in the external world, and entities as they are conventionally named and therefore categorised in the broader community (what things are called).

In this way, the adult–child talk during shared reading provides infants with subtle "lessons" in the ways experience is organised in the adult language. The experiential content of picture books for infants and toddlers is rarely random, but is usually presented according to the organisation of knowledge in the adult world. Even picture books for the youngest children tend to be organised thematically. Each page of *This Little Cat* (Horacek, 2005) depicts a different cat, accompanied by a generalised statement about its typical behaviour; for example, lying in the sun, eating fish, playing with wool, purring, and drinking milk. The last page of the picture book disrupts this established pattern by depicting a close-up picture of a tiger's face, with the text reading "this big stripy cat would like YOU for dinner" (Horacek, 2005, np). This book playfully and indirectly presents tigers and domestic cats as members of the same class despite their differences in the size, shape, and behaviours.

Furthermore, the design and content of informational picture books organises classes of entities into hierarchies of knowledge (taxonomies), either directly or indirectly. For example, animals are often classified as either farm animals or wild animals. Farm animals are further classified as herd animals or pets. In Example 5.6, the mother continues to encourage Annie to name animals, while providing additional information as she goes along.

Example 5.6

ANNIE: [*looking at pictures in a book*] Look, look. Duck.
MOTHER: Mm. That's the stork.
ANNIE: A duck! A duck!
MOTHER: A duck?
ANNIE: Yeah
MOTHER: Looks like a duck.
ANNIE: Yeah
MOTHER: But it's called a stork. Can you say that word stork?
ANNIE: [*louder*] A duck!
MOTHER: Mm. It's like a duck with long legs.
ANNIE: Yeah. Legs.
MOTHER: Mm, long legs. [*turns page*] Oh, what's that there?
ANNIE: Moon.
MOTHER: And what's that?
ANNIE: Meow.
MOTHER: Yes. A pussy cat!
ANNIE: Neigh, neigh.
MOTHER: Mm. That's a horse. What's he doing?
ANNIE: Jump, jump, jump. [*moving fingers*]
MOTHER: And what are those round things?
ANNIE: Balls.
MOTHER: Balls? Do you know what they are? Eggs.
ANNIE: Balls.

MOTHER: Eggs. The ducks have laid their eggs.
What's that?
ANNIE: ?Mole.
MOTHER: [*not understanding*] Snow? Snail?
ANNIE: Mole.
MOTHER: Polar bear?
ANNIE: Mole.
MOTHER: Mole, is it?
ANNIE: Yeah. Tree.
MOTHER: Trees? What's that?
ANNIE: Lamb
MOTHER: A lamb, that's right.

The Informative Function

Another important indicator of infants' language growth during the latter half of the second year is their realisation that language can be used to inform another person about something they did not already know. As Halliday explains, this concept "is a very sophisticated one which depends on the internalization of a whole complex set of linguistic concepts that the young child does not possess" (Halliday, 1975, p. 21). The ability to communicate "unshared" information is significant because it represents an infant's growing understanding that language can be used as an alternative to personal experience.

Case studies suggest that this emerges during pragmatic (language for doing) requests for assistance or sympathy (Painter, 1984; Torr, 1997). For example, when Annie's small wagon became wedged in some bushes, she repeated "stuck" several times while trying to extricate it, which resulted in her mother assisting her to release it. Another example occurred at around the age of 22.5 months, when Annie ran to her mother in tears. In response to being asked what happened, Annie responded "fall". In these circumstances, the information being presented was easily discernible from the context, unlike the information presented in picture books. It nevertheless provided the foundation for sharing "new" information with an addressee, thus providing them with a pathway towards the ability to engage in dialogue.

The Development of Dialogue and the Influence of Siblings

The realisation that language can be used to convey unshared information, in conjunction with the adoption of the multifunctional organisation of the adult language, means that infants are now able to engage in dialogue, such that each speaker's turn in a verbal exchange becomes the point of departure for the next speaker's turn. Once infants have learnt to engage in dialogue, it becomes possible for them to use their language to ask questions and to respond to the questions of others, which is a primary means by which language serves as a vehicle for learning and acquiring knowledge.

Unlike Nigel (Halliday, 1975) and Hal (Painter, 1984), Annie shared her home, and hence her language learning environment, with her older and more loquacious sister Clara (Torr, 1986). The language learning environment experienced by a child with siblings or similar aged peers differs from that experienced by a single child, yet much of the research on early language development, including within systemic functional linguistics, has been undertaken with singleton children interacting with their mothers.

Later-born children learn language and share their language learning environment with more verbally adept siblings, and experience less speech addressed solely to themselves (Hippe & Ramirez, 2022; Jones & Adamson, 1987). Children who are learning to talk in the same environment as siblings and peers are exposed to more overheard language, although the likelihood that overheard language provides sufficient input for children to learn to talk has been contested (Brody, 2004; Golinkoff et al., 2019; Oshima-Takane et al., 1996).

In terms of participation in dialogic-type interactions with family members, Clara indirectly provided Annie with opportunities to learn how to engage in dialogue and provide new information to those who had not shared the experience. Clara did so by modelling recounts of past experiences (Example 5.7), seeking information by asking questions (Example 5.8) and making comparisons between one aspect of experience and another (Example 5.9).

Example 5.7

FATHER: [*asking children about an outing to a farm*]
CLARA: Yeah, I holded a little chickie.
ANNIE: I hold chickie.
CLARA: And it had a little house with holes for the mouses.
FATHER: Really! And what did you see, Annie?
ANNIE: I hold chick.
CLARA: And I gave it a little tickle.
ANNIE: I tickle.
FATHER: And you tickled it too!

Example 5.8

   [*Mother and father are talking about pizza.*]

CLARA: What are pizzas?
MOTHER: They're sort of like big round pieces of bread with tomatoes and
      bacon …
FATHER: Do you think you'd like those?
ANNIE: What pizzas?
MOTHER: [*repeats explanation*]
ANNIE: Sausage, sausage.

MOTHER: No, it's not really like a sausage, no …
FATHER: But it has a sausage on it, cabanossi.
MOTHER: Oh yes, that sort of sausage.

Example 5.9

CLARA: [*spooning cottage cheese from a container into a bowl*] It looks like ice-cream.
ANNIE: [*turning to mother*] Cottage cheese look like ice-cream, Mummy.
MOTHER: Yes, it does, doesn't it?

Shared Reading with Siblings

Siblings play a powerful role in shaping the learning environment of younger children who are engaged in the process of learning to talk (Oshima-Takane & Robbins, 2003). Shared reading with a group of children of different ages affects the qualities of the learning opportunities that are available for each child. Example 5.10 provides support for the findings of Van Kleeck and Beckley-McCall (2002), who observed five mothers interacting separately with one child, and then with two differently aged children together. They found that "neither the younger nor the older child is fully supported in the simultaneous book-sharing condition" (p. 188).

Example 5.10

MOTHER: What's that in the picture, Annie?
    What's that in the picture?
CLARA: A bubby.
ANNIE: Bubby.
MOTHER: What's that?
ANNIE: Bubub.
MOTHER: That's right. It's a baby. And what's … is that a mummy?
CLARA: Yes.
MOTHER: Not a mummy.
CLARA: [*laughing*]
MOTHER: What's that?
ANNIE: Dog
CLARA: Not a baby.
MOTHER: What's that? [*pointing at baby*]
ANNIE: Bubububub.
MOTHER: Mmm. And what's that one?
ANNIE: There. There.
MOTHER: Who's that?
ANNIE: That.
MOTHER: That's the baby's Mummy. And who's that?
ANNIE: Daddy.

CLARA: [*playfully*] I think it's a doctor. It's not a bath. Not a bath.
MOTHER: [*mishearing*] It's not a bus?
CLARA: No, a bath. No, Annie said "bath".
ANNIE: [*upset, cries*]

When parents and educators attempt to read picture books with two or more differently aged young children, who have different language abilities, interests and book-sharing experiences, it is inevitable that time will be spent negotiating which books will be read. Consider Example 5.11.

Example 5.11

ANNIE: [*holds up three bears book*] Bear, bear, bear, bear.
CLARA: Annie, this is a good idea.
MOTHER: Yes, we'll have the three bears in a minute Annie. First, well, who went first yesterday? Oh, Clara went first, so we'll have three bears then teddy bears' picnic.
MOTHER: [*begins reading*] The three bears.
CLARA: Mum, Mum, Mum, are we going to read two today?
MOTHER: Yes, we're going to have two. [*reads*] Once there were three bears … And upstairs in the house there were three beds.
ANNIE: [*pointing*] There, there.
MOTHER: Yes, yes. [*reading*] She filled a great big bowl for the papa bear.
CLARA: Mum, mum. You read this too.
MOTHER: Well, I can't read them both together.
CLARA: Why?
MOTHER: Well, I've only got one tongue to talk with.
CLARA: And Mum, if you had two mouths, then you could read two books. If you had three mouths, you could talk with three mouths.
MOTHER: That's right.
ANNIE: [*pointing at a page*] There.
MOTHER: The mama bear made some porridge.
MOTHER: There's Goldilocks. Would you do that if you knocked on somebody's door and they weren't home? Just go inside?
CLARA: Yeah.
MOTHER: Would you?
CLARA: Yes.

Shared reading is a complex process in which infants who are engaged in learning one mode of meaning making (language) are simultaneously engaged in using it to construe another mode of meaning making (visual images). This learning is facilitated when adults draw connections between the child's personal experiences and the content of picture books (Blake et al., 2006), as for example in Example 5.11. Such text-to-life connections demonstrate to children that the meanings in picture books have relevance for their own lives, thus fostering the motivation to engage further with books and reading. They also at the same time show children how to "read" pictures.

Into the Mother Tongue(s)

Towards the end of infants' second year, the distinction between pragmatic and mathetic contexts begins to break down, and infants begin to reconceptualise the meaning of "function" in a more abstract sense. Whereas previously a word could either be used in the context of obtaining goods and services, or in the context of reflecting on experience, it could now be used *both* to represent experience *and* to encode speech function within the same utterance, as evidenced in Example 5.12.

Example 5.12

> Twenty-three month old Phoebe was sitting in her high chair when she noticed a bottle of milk on the bench. She said "milk" on a rising tone to request a drink of milk (=give me milk/I want milk). Her mother gave Phoebe a drink and continued preparing a meal. After finishing her drink, Phoebe placed her cup on the tray, and noticed that some drops of milk had spilt on its surface. She touched the drops with one of her fingers, and said in a falling tone "milk" (=there is some milk/I see some milk).

This small exchange was significant because Phoebe had just combined two strands of meaning simultaneously within a single utterance: the interpersonal meaning of the word as a speech act (a request or a comment) was expressed through intonation, and its representational meaning was expressed lexically (milk). This showed that Phoebe's words were becoming freed from the con-textual constraints of the previous transitional period. From about two years of age onwards, most infants begin to represent the speech function (demanding or commenting) through intonation, and experiential content lexically.

Once children begin to express both types of meaning within a single utterance, they have achieved the basic understanding that language can serve more than one function simultaneously. It is then a short step into adopting the multifunctional organisation of the adult language, according to which each complete clause simultaneously serves three different metafunctions. First, language serves as a means of representing experience (the experiential metafunction). That is, it has content; it is about something. Secondly, language serves as a means of communicating that experiential content to other speakers, referred to as the interpersonal metafunction of language. Thirdly, language serves a textual function, by knitting together the experiential and interpersonal strands of meaning expressed through the words and structures into a coherent and cohesive text.

By two years of age, children are beginning to interact with an increasingly wide circle of acquaintances. Many are attending Early Childhood Education and Care centres where they interact with adults and children with whom they are less familiar, thus creating the impetus to adopt the language of their speech community in order to participate fully in the social life around them. As Halliday (2006) explains "Some richer open-ended kind of semiotic system is needed for the child to be able to construe the complexity of his experience and enact the complexity of his interpersonal relationships. What makes such a system possible is grammar" (p. 30). As children begin to produce longer multiword utterances, they also begin to use language serving a textual function, opening up the opportunity to engage in genuine dialogue with others.

Summation: Shared Reading with Infants from 18 to 24 months

Adults can support children's language and literacy development by:

- Following the child's lead when talking about the words and pictures.
- Focusing on the achievement of shared meaning.
- Asking "what's that" questions and listening carefully to child's responses.
- Making connections between the book and the child's personal experiences.
- Describing what is happening in the pictures.
- Explaining the meanings of unfamiliar words.
- Referring to their own and the child's mental processes (thinking, wondering, knowing, remembering).
- Using gestures, voice quality, facial expressions, puppets, music and other resources to engage and sustain infants' interest and support their comprehension.
- Using book-related terminology (e.g. page, letter, illustration, author etc.).
- Reading each book more than once and having it available for later exploration by the child.

Infants contribute during shared reading by:

- Initiating shared reading by bringing books to adults to read.
- Expressing interest and pleasure in books.
- Pointing, vocalising, touching and patting the book.
- Copying actions depicted in the book (touch your toes, turn around).
- Responding to adult's question (what's that) by pointing, vocalising and/or naming.
- Chiming in with familiar refrains.
- Making animal sounds in response to pictures of animals.
- Turning the pages in books.

The book contributes to shared reading by:

- Containing topics and themes that interest children and resonate with them emotionally.

- Providing illustrations that represent diversity of culture, ethnicity, gender, age and ability.
- Being kept in good condition showing that adults value picture books.
- Containing new and interesting vocabulary.
- Containing predictable texts and literary language that children can easily remember and recite in unison.
- Making a clear distinction between the illustrations and the print.
- Containing features that encourage children to respond physically by clapping, doing finger plays, etc.

Concluding Remarks

Shared reading is an activity in which language plays a central role. Shared reading requires sustained focus on two-dimensional pictorial representations of reality that can *only* be construed by verbal interaction. This means that shared reading provides an early experience of literacy-oriented "ways of knowing" about the world that in some ways foreshadow the forms of educational knowledge that are learnt after school entry. Shared reading of picture books provides children with language learning opportunities that are associated with certain aspects of educational knowledge. These aspects include naming and classification, decontextualised language, exposure to the patterns of written text, and construing the meanings of visual images.

Listening to the print in picture books read aloud provides infants with early exposure to the patterns of written language, while the visual images, and the parent–child talk, provide additional support for the interpretation. Learning how to construe visual images through language is as important as learning how to construe experience in language. During shared reading, the pictures and print support each other, and the meanings are further supported by the adult's talk about the pictures. For some infants, shared reading plays a significant role in driving this transition by providing unique opportunities to gain new knowledge, not from lived experience or through observation or trial and error, but from shared experience with picture books. This type of experience provides the foundations for the forms of educational knowledge that are valued in school contexts.

References

Blake, J., Mcdonald, S., Bayrami, L., Agosta, V., & Milian, A. (2006). Book reading styles in dual-parent and single-mother families. *British Journal of Educational Psychology*, 76(3), 501–515. doi:10.1348/000709905X49719.

Brody, G. H. (2004). Siblings' direct and indirect contributions to child development. *Current Directions in Psychological Science*, 13(3), 124–126. doi:10.1111%2Fj.0963-7214.2004.00289.x.

Burningham, J. (1984). *Wobble pop*. Walker Books.

Christ, T., & Wang, C. (2010). Bridging the vocabulary gap: What research tells us about vocabulary instruction in early childhood. *Young Children*, 65(4), 84–91.

Clemens, L. F., & Kegel, C. (2021). Unique contribution of shared book reading on adult–child language interaction. *Journal of Child Language*, 48(2), 373–386. doi:10.1017/S0305000920000331.

Golinkoff, R. M., Hoff, E., Rowe, M. L., Tamis-LeMonda, C. S., & Hirsh-Pasek, K. (2019). Language matters: Denying the existence of the 30-million-word gap has serious consequences. *Child Development*, 90(3), 985–992 doi:10.11/cdev.13128.

Gratier, M., & Devouche, E. (2017). The development of infant participation in communication. In M. Filippa, P. Kuhn & B. Westrup (Eds.), *Early vocal contact and pre-term infant brain development* (pp. 55–68). Springer International Publishing.

Halliday, M. A. K. (1975). *Learning how to mean: Explorations in the Development of Language*. Edward Arnold.

Halliday, M. A. K. (1994). *An introduction to functional grammar* (2nd ed.). Edward Arnold.

Halliday, M. A. K. (2006). On grammar as the driving force from primary to higher-order consciousness. In G. Williams & A. Lukin (Eds.), *Development of language: Functional perspectives on species and individuals* (pp. 15–44). Bloomsbury.

Hippe, L., & Ramirez, N. (2022). Sibs and bibs: Older siblings and infant vocabulary development. In Y. Gong & F. Kpogo, (Eds.), *Proceedings of the 46th annual Boston University Conference on Language Development* (pp. 312–324). Cascadilla Press.

Horacek, P. (2005). *This little cat*. Walker Books.

Jones, C. P., & Adamson, L. B. (1987). Language use in mother–child and mother–child–sibling interactions. *Child Development*, 58(2), 356–336. doi:10.2307/1130512.

Lee, J. (2011). Size matters: Early vocabulary as a predictor of language and literacy competence. *Applied Psycholinguistics*, 32, 69–92. doi:10.1017/S0142716410000299.

Oshima-Takane, Y., & Robbins, M. (2003). Linguistic environment of secondborn children. *First Language*, 23(1), 21–40. doi:10.1177%2F0142723703023001002.

Oshima-Takane, Y., Goodz, E., & Derevensky, J. L. (1996). Birth order effects on early language development: Do secondborn children learn from overheard speech? *Child Development*, 67, 621–634. doi:10.1111/j.1467-8624.1996.tb01755.x.

Painter, C. (1984). *Into the mother tongue: A case study in early language development*. Frances Pinter.

Soderstrom, M., & Wittebolle, K. (2013). When do caregivers talk? The influences of activity and time of day on caregiver speech and child vocalizations in two childcare environments. *PLoS ONE*, 8(11): e80646. doi:10.1371/journal.pone.0080646.

Torr, J. (published as Oldenburg) (1986). The transitional stage of a second child: 18 months to 2 years. *Australian Review of Applied Linguistics*, 9(1), 123–135.

Torr, J. (1997). *From child tongue to mother tongue: A case study of language development in the first two and a half years*. Monographs in Systemic Linguistics, 9. University of Nottingham.

Van Kleeck, A., & Beckley-McCall, A. (2002). A comparison of mothers' individual and simultaneous book sharing with preschool siblings: An exploratory study of five families. *American Journal of Speech-Language Pathology*, 11, 175–189.

6 Shared Reading from Two to Three Years

Language, Literature, and Learning

This chapter will explore the ways in which toddlers' language development shapes, and is shaped by, their experiences of shared reading of picture books. Between the ages of two and three, most toddlers begin to communicate using some words and structures of the adult language. Over their third year, children continue to develop their language knowledge and skills, and shared reading provides a unique context for learning language and learning through language about the world, including the symbolic world represented in print and pictures (Halliday, 1993). Shared reading involves the complex intermingling of different semiotic systems; visual imagery, written text, and non-verbal gestures of various kinds, all mediated by the supportive presence of a parent, educator, or other caregiver. Children's developments in language provide them with a resource for exploring the meanings they encounter in picture books, which in turn builds their knowledge about the world.

Learning Language from Two to Three Years: Into the Mother Tongue

During their third year, toddlers become adept at using the language(s) of their community to interact with others (the *interpersonal metafunction* of language) and to represent their experience of the world (the *experiential metafunction* of language). They will continue to develop their language and literacy knowledge and skills for the rest of their lives. Halliday (1975) explains that, although toddlers have crossed an important threshold, they still have much to learn:

> his entry into Phase III, at about the end of his second year, does not mean that he has mastered the English language. It means that he has constructed for himself a three-level semiotic system which is organized the way the adult language is. ... But it still has a long way to go before it comes into full flower.
>
> (Halliday, 1975, p. 115)

Shared reading of picture books plays a vital role in facilitating this blossoming. From about 18 to 24 months, many infants make a distinction between words

DOI: 10.4324/9781003168812-6

used to seek goods and services (a pragmatic "language for doing" function) and words used to name aspects of their environment (a mathetic "language for learning" function). But the same word could not be used to serve both functions.

During their third year, however, these distinctions disappear as toddlers realise that all complete sentences function *both* to encode speech function, through the systems of Mood and Modality, *and* to represent experience, through the systems of Transitivity. This realisation inevitably leads toddlers to engage in longer conversations with others, thus facilitating the emergence of a third function of language (the Textual metafunction). This function enables speakers to create cohesive stretches of text and to relate their utterances to the preceding ones and to the non-linguistic setting in which they are uttered. Toddlers' recognition that they can "mean" more than one thing at a time opens up new possibilities for using language as a resource for learning more generally. The three processes, learning language, learning through language, and learning about language, are inextricably connected (Halliday, 1993).

Developments in the Experiential Metafunction

The experiential metafunction is realised grammatically in Transitivity, which provides toddlers with a resource for representing their understanding of "reality" in terms of processes (verbal groups), the actors engaged in the processes (nominal groups) and the circumstances involved in the processes (mainly adjectives and adverbs) (Halliday & Hasan, 1989). Children in their third year are able to construe the world around them in terms of material, mental and relational processes. Initially, young children use mental processes with first person subjects only (Torr, 1998), perhaps because toddlers are still developing a concept of *mind mindedness* (Degotardi & Torr, 2007); that is, the understanding that others engage in mental processes that cannot be seen, only inferred as taking place. For example, at this age toddlers are beginning to construe themselves as engaging in the mental processes of liking and wanting, but cannot yet conceive of them as occurring in others.

Shared reading of picture books provides toddlers with many opportunities to begin to understand that they, and other people, engage in mental processes. Parents and educators have multiple opportunities to refer to mental processes, by referring to the mental processes of the represented characters in simple narratives, and also to the toddler's own participation as a thinker, knower and reader (see Example 6.1).

Example 6.1

   [*Catherine, 36 months old, and her mother are looking at a page in a book.*]

MOTHER: Do you know what that building is?
CATHERINE: What?
MOTHER: See the building in the picture?

CATHERINE: What?
MOTHER: It's the Opera House.
CATHERINE: We did saw that when … when … when we saw the race.
MOTHER: That's right.

In Example 6.2, an educator and two toddlers are reading the picture book *Maisy's Plane* (Cousins, 2014). Within each illustration is a picture of bird. The bird does not play a role in the narrative, but it appears in the background on several pages.

Example 6.2

EDUCATOR: [*turning back through the pages*] Can you remember where that bird was before? Can you see the little bird? He was right back here. [*pointing*] He was still there [*turning page and pointing*]. There *was* a little bird. I wonder what happened to the little bird.
CHARLIE: [*pointing*] Cheep cheep.
EDUCATOR: Do you wonder? I was wondering if that little bird was going to get to the party.
ALEX: Yes.
EDUCATOR: Do you think he got to the party? Let's see if he followed.

(Torr, 2020, p. 132)

In Example 6.2, the educator verbalises her own mental processes as *wondering* and *seeing*. She uses questioning to gauge the child's understanding of the text, prefacing her questions with the mental processes *remember, see, wonder*, and *think*. In this way, the educator positions the child in her speech as one who also engages in mental processes. The educator thus construes reading as an interpretive process requiring mental activity of various kinds. She also demonstrates that one cannot know another person's mental activity unless he or she verbally expresses it. The educator indirectly demonstrates that learning is not simply a process of receiving a body of facts transmitted by an expert, but rather a process of interpretation in which different perspectives are possible.

Developments in the Interpersonal Metafunction

The interpersonal metafunction is realised grammatically in the systems of Mood and Modality (Halliday & Hasan, 1989). Mood is expressed through the placement of the subject and finite elements of a clause. The development of the Mood system provides toddlers with a resource for exchanging meanings with other speakers. By their third year, many toddlers use language to ask and respond to questions, make statements, and direct the behaviour of others. Their emerging Mood system enables toddlers to engage in dialogue, such that each speaker's turn in a conversation becomes the point of departure for the next turn. In this way, through conversations with more knowledgeable others, toddlers are able to use their language to share their ideas and feelings, seek new information, and grow their knowledge about the world. Initially, some children "practise" dialogue by requesting that the adult ask them a known-answer question (Example 6.3).

Example 6.3

CATHERINE: Mummy, say "what was in the dark dark cupboard".
MOTHER: What was in the dark dark cupboard?
CATHERINE: A little tiny mouse!

Almost as soon as toddlers gain control of some features of the Mood system, they begin to invert playfully the role of "questioner" and "responder". Example 6.4 presents a conversation between toddler Zoe and her educator in her Early Childhood Education and Care centre. Zoe is using her questioning not to gain unknown information, but rather to enjoy playing the role of "questioner" during shared focus on a familiar picture book.

Example 6.4

ZOE: Read a book? [*pointing to cover*] what's that?
EDUCATOR: It says "Goodnight". The mummy's giving the little boy a hug.
ZOE: [*pointing to another picture*] What's that?
EDUCATOR: [*reads*] "I like soft warm towels".
ZOE: What's that?
EDUCATOR: That's the little girl. She's having a bath.
ZOE: What's that?
EDUCATOR: I think that might be her teddy. [*reading*] "I can put on my
    pyjamas".
ZOE: What's that?
EDUCATOR: That's the little boy putting on his pyjamas.
ZOE: [*pointing*] What's that?
EDUCATOR: [*reading*] "And comb my hair all by myself".
ZOE: What's that?
EDUCATOR: The little girl's combing her hair.
ZOE: What's that?
EDUCATOR: Having some dinner. "Good. It's my bedtime snack. I'm hungry."
ZOE: No! Morning tea!
EDUCATOR: Is it morning tea?
ZOE: Yes.
ALEX: Dinner!
ZOE: ?the book.
EDUCATOR: Dinner? Alex thinks it might be dinner. And Zoe thinks it is
    morning tea. The little boy's having something to eat.

In Example 6.5, 30 month old Annie is deploying her Mood system to seek knowledge about the meanings in the illustrations of a picture book (Torr, 1997, p. 206). She uses her language to seek the name of an entity (*WH question*), confirmation of her interpretation (*a yes/no question*) and an explanation (*WH question*). The child is not simply seeking a label, as in earlier phases of development, but rather is seeking to understand how one element in an illustration relates to another.

Example 6.5

> [*Annie and her mother are reading a picture book*]

ANNIE: What's that?
MOTHER: A little girl.
ANNIE: [*referring to an incident on the previous page*] That go girl ... that tiny girl go there (as) well?
MOTHER: Yes, she's there too.
ANNIE: [*referring to a story read several hours earlier*] Why King write Abu on elephant?

The term "modality" refers to expressions which convey a speaker's evaluation concerning the possibility that a certain state of affairs will occur, or the obligations involved in a particular situation (Halliday, 1994). Modality is expressed by the modal verbs *can/could, may/might, will/would, should, must, ought to, need to, has to*, and adjuncts such as *perhaps* and *usually*. Modality provides children with a resource for learning how to predict and hypothesise and to recognise that their perspective may not be shared by others. It also provides children with a resource for exploring social behaviours, concepts of politeness, moral values and so on. Modality is a complex part of the grammar that continues to develop throughout the school age ranges. It expresses subtle shades of meaning and is important in the construal of educational knowledge at school.

By three years of age, some children have begun to express degrees of *possibility* and *certainty* that a certain state of affairs may occur, by using projections (Halliday, 1994). The term *projection* refers to a particular kind of relationship between two or more clauses. The secondary clause is "projected" through a primary "projecting" clause, either as a thought (I think + clause) or as a saying (She said + clause) (Halliday 1994). This kind of complex clause structure often occurs in the talk of parents, educators and young children during shared reading of picture books, as demonstrated in Example 6.5 (Torr, 1997, p. 215).

Example 6.5

> [*Catherine, younger sister Annie and mother are reading an informational book about wild cats. The printed text refers to "a spotted wild cat", but there is no accompanying picture.*]

CATHERINE: What does the spotted wild cat look like?
MOTHER: I think it looks like an ordinary cat.

ANNIE: I think that cat on another page.

MOTHER: You think so? We'll see a wild cat on another page? Well, let's just see. [*she turns back through the pages to look for it*]

The likely appearance of the wild cat, and the possibility that a picture of one may be located on a different page, are expressed in the talk of the mother and Annie using projecting clauses. Catherine's question reveals her awareness that the printed text and the illustrations are related to each other in a non-arbitrary way. The children's responses in Example 6.5 reveal their awareness that knowledge as presented in such picture books is organised in certain ways.

Mental Processes, Projection and Social Positioning

The frequency and qualities of the adult–child talk during shared reading are associated with the social positioning of families. Projecting clause complexes such as in Example 6.5 are more likely to occur during adult–child talk when the parent (typically the mother) is highly educated (van Kleeck, 2014) and/or is employed in a position involving a high degree of autonomy (Hasan, 1991; Williams, 1999, 2001). As van Kleeck (2014) explains "The more education a child's mother has, the more likely she is to use a school-like or academic register with her child when at home, even when engaged in everyday living activities" (p. 725). By academic register, van Kleeck (2014) is referring to talk that is not reliant on the immediate context for its interpretation, which encourages the child's sense of autonomy, refers to the child's states of consciousness, asks the child to verbally display their knowledge and to engage in reasoning. The use of mental processes subtly indicates that different perspectives on the same phenomenon are possible, thus providing an early experience of one of the features of an academic register (van Kleeck, 2014). It has been proposed that frequent experiences of this type of academic talk orient infants and toddlers to "ways of knowing" about their world that resonate with the requirements of formal schooling (Heath, 1983; Michaels, 1981; Hasan, 1991, 1992).

Developments in the Textual Metafunction

As children gain facility in using language to engage with others, they also begin to produce certain forms of language that serve a third, Textual, metafunction. As the name suggests, the textual metafunction is involved in the creation of cohesive text beyond the level of the sentence or clause. The ability to engage in dialogue, where one utterance provides the point of departure for the next utterance, requires a speaker to make connections using grammatical resources such as pronouns, conjunctions, and ellipses (Halliday & Hasan, 1989). The textual metafunction is also involved in the presentation of information within the clause, as the first element provides the point of departure for the rest of the clause. Typically, the first element presents "given" information that the speaker perceives to be known to the addressee, followed by "new" information considered to be unshared by the addressee. From the ages of two to three, many children create cohesion by listing related entities in a sequence, and in Examples 6.6 (Torr, 1997, p. 190) and 6.7, as a pathway into representing cohesion using the conventional resources of the adult grammar.

Example 6.6

   [*Mother and Annie are looking at a night-time scene in a picture book.*]

MOTHER: Do you think it is daytime or night-time?
ANNIE: Night-time.
MOTHER: That's right! How do you know it's night-time?
ANNIE: Moon (in the) sky. Stars (are) there. Dark night-time. Birds night-time.
   Moon. Stars. Moon. Stars there. Up there.
MOTHER: Mm. All these things happen in the night-time.

Example 6.7

ANNIE: [*looking at a picture in her picture book*] House?
MOTHER: House, yes.
ANNIE: Cat. Owls. Beetle. Mouse. House. Owl. Flowers there.

Toddlers' Use of Language as a Vehicle for Learning

The language features of shared reading change as toddlers become more skilled at using language to represent experience, interact with others, and engage in dialogue. Each development in toddlers' linguistic repertoires provides them with a resource for making meaning during the shared reading of picture books. In the process of constructing their language and using it to learn about the world, toddlers draw selectively on the types of meanings being expressed by those around them in their environment, and then focus on those meanings that are most salient to them at a particular stage of their learning and development. While infants' earliest experiences of shared reading typically involve them responding to parents' and educators' questioning (*What's that? Where's the duck?*), by three years of age many toddlers are actively using their linguistic resources to seek information and gain knowledge about the world. The child's active pursuit of knowledge can be seen in Example 6.8.

Example 6.8

CLARA: [*looking at picture*] What's that?
MOTHER: It's called a corkscrew.
CASSIE: Corkscrew.
MOTHER: Do you know what that's for? Can you guess? Tell Mummy.
CASSIE: No! I don't know.

MOTHER: A corkscrew. It's taking the cork out of bottles. Sometimes bottles have a cork in them to seal them.

Shared Reading as a Vehicle for Learning

Toddlers' Interpersonal Strategies for Learning

An awareness of the semantic content of young children's questions can provide insights into their ways of thinking and learning during shared reading. Hasan (1991; 1996) made a distinction between three types of questions on the basis of their semantic patterning and the nature of the information sought from the addressee. *Confirm* (polar or yes/no) questions seek either a confirmation or a denial from the addressee. *Specify* (who, what, where, when) questions seek the name of a person, location, entity or time. *Explain* (how, why) questions seek an explanation from the addressee. Most toddlers' questions seek the name of an object or entity, although many parents and educators respond not only with a name, but use the toddlers' specify questions as a point of departure for providing additional information, explanations and descriptions in relation to the words, pictures, and the world more generally, as in Example 6.9.

Example 6.9

CASSIE: What's that?
MOTHER: That's a special knife.
CASSIE: No.
MOTHER: No? What is it then?
CASSIE: To get bindis [*a prickly weed*] out.
MOTHER: To get bindis out? Like tweezers?
CASSIE: Yes. And scissors.

Toddlers' Experiential Strategies for Learning

According to Halliday (1994), the experiential metafunction of language "enables human beings to build a mental picture of reality, to make sense of what goes on around and inside them" (p. 106). Having adopted the metafunctional organisation of the adult language, toddlers become more adept at using their language skills as a vehicle for learning more generally. Both adults and toddlers employ a number of semiotic strategies to construe the meanings they encounter during shared reading (Torr, 2004). The development of naming (lexis), for example, provides toddlers with a powerful resource for learning. Toddlers frequently respond to an entity depicted in an illustration by naming it, as in Example 6.7, in which Annie responds to an illustration by naming the entities depicted in the illustration. Some toddlers extend on naming by describing their observations using clause-like structures.

Comparison as a learning strategy involves the use of analogy to classify phenomena by comparing an action or entity depicted in a picture book with the toddler's own personal lived experience; for example, when Annie fell off a chair she said "fell down wall ... like Tom Kitten", referencing a situation depicted in one of her favourite picture books. Generalisation is a learning strategy during which a toddler observes an entity in a picture, and then builds on that specific observation to make a more general statement (generalisation) about experience (a characteristic of informational registers). See Example 6.10 (Torr, 1997, p. 209).

Example 6.10

> [*Ariana and her mother are looking at pictures of frogs and tadpoles in a book*]

ARIANA: Tiny eyes!
MOTHER: Tiny eyes, yes. Do you know what they are called?
ARIANA: Oh?
MOTHER: Tadpoles.
ARIANA: Tadpoles (are) like fish, Mummy.

In Example 6.11, Annie has noticed that, in a picture of a duck in profile, only one eye is visible. Based on her understanding that, like all creatures, ducks have two eyes, she uses her linguistic resources to solve an apparent disparity between her current knowledge and the depiction of the duck in the picture (Torr, 1997, p. 205).

Example 6.11

> [*Mother and Annie are doing a wooden jigsaw puzzle together. The paper on top of the duck piece has been torn off. The mother attempts to draw a new duck on top of the wooden piece.*]

MOTHER: [*talking as she draws the duck*] It'll need a beak, won't it? And its head ... we'll do an eye ... its coat. There we are ... it's all fixed up now.
ANNIE: There beak. Where eye two?
MOTHER: What darling?
ANNIE: Where other eye?
MOTHER: [*not understanding at first*] Another eye? Oh no, it only needs ... the other eye's over on the other side of its head and we can't see its other side.
ANNIE: Other eye ... head.
MOTHER: Mm. Look, I'll show you with ... what can I show you with? Here, see this toy duck [*holding a rubber toy*] see ... you can only see one eye when I hold it like that. If you turn it around you can see the other eye.
ANNIE: Other eye. See other eye. See other side. Other eye. See other eye.

Ways of Speaking: The Development of Register

As they learn to communicate with other people using their mother tongue(s), children also at the same time learn how to vary their language in predictable ways according to the functions it serves in their social and intellectual life. Dickinson et al. (2014) explains that "Registers are identifiable by specific linguistic features and functions, and different registers are used for different intellectual and social purposes" (p. 232). Picture books provide young children with exposure to the language patterns of different registers (sometimes referred to as genres) including narrative, recount, poetry and drama. Infants and toddlers begin to gain experience with the language of different registers through the use of language serving an imaginative function.

Pretend Play

The imaginative function is initially realised through pretend play, which provides a fertile environment for toddlers to use language as they adopt different character roles. Toddlers enjoy making sounds as they pretend to be animals, robots, helicopters, fire engines and so on. Toddlers' pretend play often involves the reconstruction of familiar scenarios. Annie used pretend play to explore the different ways in which mothers and babies interact with each other, as she adopted the "voices" of the mother and baby. Please see Example 6.12 (Torr, 1997, p. 192).

Example 6.12

> [*Annie, 25 months old, is playing alone in her bedroom with her doll.*]
> [*Pretending to be crying baby*] Boo hoo hoo.
> [*Normal voice*] Baby sad.
> [*Baby "voice"*] I wet. I bang head.
> [*Normal voice*] My baby sore, cry.
> [*"Mother" voice, slowly to doll*] There there …poor little thing.
> [*Patting doll*] Sh, sh. Poor baby.

Pretend play and language play are closely related. As soon as a grammatical system is productive in a child's language, it may be manipulated for playful and imaginative purposes. Case studies show young children deliberately misnaming objects in picture books for humorous effect (Torr & Simpson, 2003), as in Example 6.13.

Example 6.13

> Toby (1:10) and his mother are looking at a picture book together. Toby points to an illustration of a piece of cheese and says "butter". His mother says "no, it's cheese". Toby, smiling broadly, repeats the word "butter".
>
> (Torr & Simpson, 2003, p. 177)

Examples of toddlers deliberately misnaming objects have also been observed by Dunn (1988). Such jokes are a conscious distortion of reality, and suggest an early awareness of the perspective of another, as they rely on the understanding that the mother's perspective is not the same as the child's. This form of language play may relate to later literacy development by orienting the child to the potential of language to be used metaphorically, which is fundamental to poetry, narrative, drama, film and so on. Crystal (1996) has linked language play to future success in learning to read.

Recount

Many picture books for infants and toddlers present information in the form of a recount. A recount consists of a retelling of events that happened in the past, usually as a sequence that unfolds in chronological order. A personal evaluation or comment about the events may be stated at the end. As toddlers come to understand that language can be used to tell another person something they do not already know (the informative function of language), they become more skilled at recounting experience not shared with the addressee. Please see Example 6.14 in which Ariana is attempting to recount a recent experience.

Example 6.14

> [*Ariana is getting ready to have a bath. The soap has a picture of a cat imprinted on it.*]

ARIANA: That ... that pussycat soap.
MOTHER: Who bought it for you?
ARIANA: Um ... um ... Granny bought me.
MOTHER: Granny bought it for you, that's right.
ARIANA: Yes. At shop, shop today. At shop ... at shop today.
MOTHER: At the shop today?
ARIANA: Yeah.
MOTHER: It wasn't today, it was a little while ago, wasn't it?
ARIANA: Rub rub rub rub rub.
MOTHER: Mm. Rub rub with the soap.
ARIANA: Mummy, people lie down ... bath.
MOTHER: Mm, they do, don't they?

Shared Reading with a Toddler: A Snapshot

While many toddlers enjoy the aesthetic experience of looking at the pictures in picture books, the experience of *talking* about the visual images and written text draws their attention to the fact that meanings are expressed both within each page and also across all the pages in the picture book as a whole. During their third year, toddlers play an active role in construing the meanings they encounter in the words and pictures. Toddlers' verbal contributions during shared reading can reveal much about their understanding of their social, inner, external and symbolic worlds, and provide insights into which books will be most relevant to them at particular phases in their learning.

Example 6.15 presents a shared reading episode between 26 month old Clara and her mother. They are reading a simple text, *The Friend* (Burningham, 1975), comprising just eight double-page spreads. The small amount of printed text is presented on the left hand side of each page, with a corresponding illustration on the right hand side. The book is one of Clara's favourites.

Example 6.15

MOTHER: You ready?

CLARA: Yes.

MOTHER: "The Friend". [*pointing to cover*] It's a little boy and his friend, and they've got a teddy. And do you know what his friend's name is? Remember?

CLARA: [*attempting to pronounce*] Arf

MOTHER: Arthur.

CLARA: [*attempting*] Arfer

MOTHER: [*pointing to small illustration on title page*] Here they are, playing in the garden. [*turns page*] "Arthur is my friend". He's got a trolley like yours. And he's taking his teddy for a ride in his trolley. [*turns page*] "We always play together".

CLARA: [*pointing*] Look.

MOTHER: Mmm.

CLARA: A bucket.

MOTHER: Mm. A bucket, that's right. [*turns page*] "We play outside when it's fine". Now, they're having a good play outside. [*turns page*] "And stay inside when it is raining". [*pause. turns page*] "Sometimes I don't like Arthur". Uh oh. What's happening here?

CLARA: Fight with Arthur.

MOTHER: Mm. What are they fighting about?

CLARA: Teddy.

MOTHER: Mm. They both want teddy. What do you think they should do? Do you think they should take it in turns?

CLARA: [*nods*]

MOTHER: That'd be best, wouldn't it? [*turns page*] "So Arthur goes home". [*turns page*] "Then I'm by myself". Do you think he's happy or sad?

CLARA: [*whispering*] Sad.

MOTHER: Mm. That's what I think too. [*turns page*] "I have other friends of course". What's this little girl doing?

CLARA: [*whispering*] Going walk.

MOTHER: Mm. Going for a walk. That's right. And this girl's got a skipping rope. Why are you whispering, love? [*both laugh*] You can talk louder if you like?

CLARA: [*shouts*] Mummy! [*both laugh again.*]

MOTHER: Looks like he's going to have a turn with the skipping rope, is he? [*turns page*] "But Arthur is my best friend". Look, they've got their arms around each other, because they're friends again. And that's the end of the story.

CLARA: [*loudly*] Again! [*Mother reads the book again*]

This book addresses a topic that resonates deeply with young children and adults alike; that is, the nature of friendship, how to connect with others, how to deal with conflict, and how to forgive. The first person narrator, a little boy, speaks directly to the child reader (Clara), who is looking at the pictures while listening to the words read aloud. The unnamed narrator reflects on his relationship with his friend Arthur. His reflections are presented in a sequence of statements using the simple everyday vocabulary of a young child. Relational processes of the identifying intensive type connect the two friends (*Arthur is my best friend*) and material processes represent the actions they do together (*play, stay inside, fight, go*). The only mental process is one of the affective type (*don't like*). The timeless present tense is used to express the ongoing continuity of the relationship.

In contrast to the first person perspective of the narrator, expressed through the printed text, the illustrations position the reader/viewer as an observer looking on, just a short distance from the two children. The children are depicted in soft pastel colouring in the centre of each page, against a plain white background. Several of the illustrations depict the little boys very close to each other or touching. Their consequent falling-out over the teddy is made explicit visually, as the boys are depicted standing apart.

The talk that occurs between Clara and her mother during the shared reading serves a pedagogical function, above and beyond the simple enjoyment of the shared attention to the text. First, the mother provides an orientation by opening the picture book to the title page and pointing out the three elements that are central to the text's meaning (*there's a little boy and his friend and they've got a teddy*).

Secondly, the mother provides an opportunity for Clara to verbally display her understanding of the text, by asking her to name the narrator's friend (*Arthur*) and to explain what happens in the text. Having heard the story many times before, Clara names the friend, explains that the argument is about possession of the teddy, that the little boy is sad after Arthur goes home, and that the little girl in the picture is going for a walk.

Thirdly, the mother makes a direct connection between the meanings in the illustrations and Clara's own life experience (*he's got a trolley like yours*). She is suggesting that the meanings in picture books relate to one's personal life. Clara is then asked to identify and empathise with the boy's feelings, which may explain why she whispered the word "sad".

Finally, the mother asks Clara what she thinks about issues arising in the text (*What do you think they should do? Do you think they should take it in turns? Do you think he's happy or sad*) thus construing Clara as a thinker who is (potentially) able to verbalise her thoughts. The mother then makes visible her own thoughts (*That's what I think too*). In this way the mother is encouraging her daughter to be verbally explicit. She is thus providing early experience in producing decontextualised language in a supportive face-to-face context.

At the end of the narrative, the mother provides a coda (*they've got their arms around each other, because they're friends again*). She uses a clause complex to make verbally explicit the reasoning behind the claim that the boys are best friends again. In many respects the mother's extra-textual talk has the features of what van Kleeck (2014) describes as academic talk. This type of talk contrasts with casual talk, which is typical of the everyday interactions that form the ebb and flow of family life.

Clara's one initiating utterance (*a bucket*) received an acknowledgement from her mother (*a bucket, that's right*). She did not elaborate, however, perhaps because the bucket does not play a significant role in construing the overall meanings in the picture book. Its presence is tangential to understanding the thematic content.

Hasan (1985) draws attention to the ways in which young children's responses to texts vary according to their age, interests, feelings and other factors:

> the growing person's own growth interacts with the language of the text; different degrees of the understanding of language, of the world around one and of the art forms in question affect the manner in which one approaches what might be described as physically the same text. Interpretation is a relatively open-ended activity, the limits on which are not set entirely by the text itself, but also by those who participate in the text. How exactly the meaning of the words would be understood depends, within general limits, upon who does the understanding.
>
> (Hasan, 1985, p. 26)

Each and every shared reading experience will differ in some way, even when the picture book is already familiar. This is partly because the illustrations in children's picture books depict many more details than are referred to in the printed text. The learning potentiality of shared reading is subtle and indirect. Concepts are learnt gradually over the early childhood years, during countless pleasant and interesting encounters with words, pictures and books.

Summation: Shared Reading from 24 to 36 months

Adults can support children's language and literacy development by:

- Reading picture books of different registers including narratives, recounts, informational books, poetry.
- Providing toddlers with a range of books on different topics and illustrative styles.

- Monitoring toddlers' understanding by asking how and why questions, and providing explanations about the meanings of words and pictures.
- Asking toddlers to predict what will happen next.
- Using book-related terminology like author, illustrator, title, and explaining what it means in context.
- Talking about the actions, motives, and feelings of the characters.
- Relating the content of the picture book to the child's own life experiences.
- Providing illustrations that represent diversity of culture, ethnicity, gender, age and ability.
- Making connections between this book and other books.
- Providing opportunities for toddlers to interact with them one to one during shared reading.

Toddlers contribute during shared reading by:

- Asking what how and why questions.
- Turning the pages of the book.
- Relating the events in the book to their personal experiences.
- Making connections between this book and other books, movies, and games.
- Retelling what happened in the story.

The book contributes to the extra-textual talk by:

- Stimulating the toddler's curiosity.
- Addressing themes that are significant to toddlers.
- Providing positive messages that encourage empathy and resilience.
- Using playful, memorable language that is easy for toddlers to remember.
- Depicting characters and situations with which toddlers can identify.

Concluding Remarks

By three years of age, most toddlers have learnt to use the language(s) of their community to represent their experiences, to engage in dialogue with others, and to create stretches of cohesive text. Reading and talking about picture books with infants and toddlers provides a language-rich experience that facilitates various aspects of language development and provides a resource for building background knowledge, comprehension of language, vocabulary and inferencing skills, all of which are necessary for children to gain access to educational knowledge and achieve success in learning to read after school entry.

References

Burningham, J. (1975). *The friend.* Jonathan Cape.

Cousins, L. (2014). *Maisy's plane.* Walker Books.

Crystal, D. (1996). Language play and linguistic intervention. *Child Language Teaching and Therapy,* 12(3), 257–379. doi: 10.1177/026565909601200307.

Degotardi, S., & Torr, J.(2007). A longitudinal investigation of mothers' mind-related talk to their 12-to 24-month-old infants. *Early Child Development and Care,* 177(6–7), 767–780. doi:10.1080/03004430701379280.

Dickinson, D., Hofer, K. G., Barnes, E. M., & Grifenhagen, J. F. (2014). Examining teachers' language in Head Start classrooms from a systemic linguistics approach. *Early Childhood Research Quarterly,* 29(3), 231–244. doi:10.1016/j.ecresq.2014.02.006.

Dunn, J. (1988). *The beginnings of social understanding.* Blackwell.

Halliday, M. A. K. (1975). *Learning how to mean: Explorations in the development of language.* Edward Arnold.

Halliday, M. A. K. (1993). Towards a language-based theory of learning. *Linguistics and Education,* 5(2): 93–116.

Halliday, M. A. K. (1994). *Introduction to functional grammar* (2nd ed.). Edward Arnold.

Halliday, M. A. K., & Hasan, R. (1989). *Language, context, and text: Aspects of language in a social-semiotic perspective* (2nd ed.). Oxford University Press.

Hasan, R. (1985). *Linguistics, language and verbal art.* Deakin University Press.

Hasan, R. (1991). Questions as a mode of learning in everyday talk. In T. Le & M. McCausland (Eds.), *Language education: Interaction and development* (Proceedings of the International Conference, Vietnam) (pp. 70–119). University of Tasmania.

Hasan, R. (1992). Rationality in everyday talk: From process to system. In J. Svartik (Ed.), *Directions in corpus linguistics* (pp. 309–344). Mouton de Gruyter.

Hasan, R. (1996). Semantic networks: A tool for the analysis of meaning. In C. Cloran, D. Butt & G. Williams (Eds.), *Ways of saying, ways of meaning. Selected papers of Ruqaiya Hasan* (pp. 104–131). Cassell.

Heath, S. (1983). *Ways with words: Ethnography of communication in communities and classrooms.* Cambridge University Press.

Michaels, S. (1981). "Sharing time": Children's narrative styles and differential access to literacy. *Language in Society,* 10 (3), 423–442. www.jstor.org/stable/4167263.

Torr, J. (1997). *From child tongue to mother tongue: A case study of language development in the first two and a half years.* Monographs in Systemic Linguistics, 9. University of Nottingham.

Torr, J. (1998). The development of modality in the preschool years: Language as a vehicle for understanding possibilities and obligations in everyday life. *Functions of Language,* 5 (2), 157–178.

Torr, J. (2004). Talking about picture books: The influence of maternal education on four- year-old children's talk with mothers and pre-school teachers. *Journal of Early Childhood Literacy,* 4 (2), 181–210. doi:10.1177/1468798404044515.

Torr, J. (2020). Shared reading as a practice for fostering early learning in an Early Childhood Education and Care centre: A naturalistic, comparative study of one infant's experiences with two educators. *Literacy,* 132–142. doi:10.1111/lit.12227.

Torr, J., & Simpson, A. (2003). The emergence of grammatical metaphor: Literacy- oriented expressions in the everyday speech of young children. In A.M. Simon- Vandenbergen, M. Taverniers & L. Ravelli (Eds.), *Grammatical metaphor: Views from systemic functional linguistics* (pp. 169–184). John Benjamins.

van Kleeck, A. (2014). Distinguishing between casual talk and academic talk beginning in the preschool years: An important consideration for speech-language pathologists. *American Journal of Speech-Language Pathology*, 23, 724–741. doi:10.1044/2014_AJSLP-14-0032.

Williams, G. (1999). The pedagogic device and the production of pedagogic discourse: A case study in early literacy education. In F. Christie (Ed.), *Pedagogy and the shaping of consciousness: Linguistic and social processes* (pp. 88–122). Cassell.

Williams, G. (2001). Literacy pedagogy prior to schooling: Relations between social positioning and semantic variation. In A. Morais, I. Neves, B. Davies & H. Baillie (Eds.), *Towards a sociology of pedagogy: The contribution of Basil Bernstein to research* (pp. 17–45).

7 Shared Reading with Infants and Toddlers in Early Childhood Education and Care Centres

The term *shared reading* in this chapter refers to the interactions between an educator and one or more children aged younger than three years as they jointly focus on, and talk about, the illustrations and words in a picture book. Shared reading in this context can be thought of as a triangle. In one corner is the picture book, which expresses its meanings through the interaction between the words and the pictures. In the second corner is the educator, who reads the print aloud and facilitates the children's understanding of the meanings through her questions and comments. In the third corner is the child or group of children, who participate in the telling by touching, pointing, vocalising, and gazing at the pictures, and listening to the patterning of the words as they are read aloud. Each corner interacts with the other two, thus each shared reading experience creates fresh and novel opportunities for learning language and constructing new knowledge.

Much of our knowledge about the educational benefits of shared reading with infants and toddlers derives from studies of mothers interacting one-to-one with their singleton child (Hirsh-Pasek et al., 2015; Weisleder & Fernald, 2013; Zimmerman et al., 2009). These studies have yielded valuable insights into the language and literacy learning opportunities that accrue to those children who have plentiful experiences with books and reading. Abundant research reveals that the frequency and qualities of shared reading with children aged under three years is strongly associated with their future language knowledge and skills as far ahead as the primary school age ranges (Shahaeian et al., 2018) even after controlling for socioeconomic background and other factors (Demir-Lira et al., 2019).

The Language Learning Environment in Early Childhood Education and Care centres

The language environment in Early Childhood Education and Care (ECEC) centres differs from that in the home, in ways that influence how shared reading is enacted. Infants and toddlers in ECEC centres spend many of their waking hours in the company of similar aged peers and various adults, including their educators, other staff, visitors, and the parents of other infants. Furthermore, unlike parents,

DOI: 10.4324/9781003168812-7

educators of children from birth to three years are required to have a professional teaching qualification, to follow an early childhood curriculum or learning framework, and to comply with government-mandated regulations (OECD, 2017). These factors all serve to shape the qualities of the teaching and learning environment, with implications for the language learning opportunities afforded by shared reading and other activities.

As is the case in all situations in which language plays a role, there is a relationship between certain features of the (non-linguistic) material situation within which shared reading takes place, and the language produced by the educators and children during the shared focus on the picture book text. Systemic functional linguistic theory (SFL) (Halliday, 1994) provides a framework for interpreting which elements in any learning environment influence the types of verbal behaviour that can potentially occur. An understanding of the relationship between language and context can support educators in planning and implementing enjoyable, language-rich experiences which facilitate children's language and literacy development. This chapter will explore how the features of the *context of situation* (Halliday & Hasan, 1989) in Early Childhood Education and Care centres influence and shape the meanings that can be realised during shared reading.

Several empirical studies have confirmed what many educators intuitively know from their professional experience; that is, that the qualities of the language addressed to children in ECEC centres relates to their current and future language and literacy outcomes (Rudd et al., 2008). A large scale longitudinal study investigated the relationship between the qualities of educators' speech in ten Early Childhood Education and Care centres and children's language skills (NICHD ECCRN, 2000). The 595 participating children had all spent more than 30 hours per week in childcare by the age of seven months. The children's expressive vocabulary (the words they can say) and comprehension (the words they understand) were assessed when they were 15 months, 24 months, and 36 months of age. The language used by the educators when addressing the children was evaluated using a composite measure referred to as "language stimulation" and defined as talk that "asks questions of child, responds to children's vocalisations, and other (nonnegative) talk to child" (NICHD ECCRN, 2000, p. 968).

The findings of this study revealed a relationship between the language stimulation provided by the educators and the children's expressive vocabulary at the three different age points. The researchers concluded that "the more that childcare environments are characterised by caregiver–child interactions that are both supportive and verbally stimulating, the better children perform" (p. 977). This study was significant because it showed empirically that the language used by educators when talking to infants and toddlers has a direct effect on children's language development. The NICHD ECCRN (2000) study focused on the language environment as a whole, rather than specifically on the qualities of shared reading of picture books within that environment.

Shared Reading in Early Childhood Education and Care centres

Informed by the findings of recent cutting-edge research and data analysis, the Infant/Toddler Environment Rating Scale (ITERS-3) (Harms et al., 2017) provides a tool for evaluating the qualities of the learning environment in early childhood infant and toddler rooms. The section titled "Language and Books" is highlighted as one of the six key areas that contribute to the overall quality of infant and toddler programs provided in ECEC centres, thus reinforcing the centrally important role played by educators in talking, listening and reading books with infants and toddlers for their overall development. A particularly beneficial feature of the ITERS-3 is that it includes examples of the types of educator practices that facilitate infants' and toddlers' communication skills, vocabulary development, and interest in books and reading.

Shared reading with infants and toddlers attending Early Childhood Education and Care centres is vital for many reasons. During shared reading, children experience more talk, and richer talk, from their educators than they do in any other activity. Soderstrom and Wittebolle (2013) recorded the naturally occurring speech produced and heard by 11 children aged between 12–29 months. Six children were recorded in their childcare centres, six were recorded at home, and one was recorded in both contexts. The amount of talk heard by the children during various activities was quantified. The study found that, although the children engaged in book-focused activities for less than 2% of their total time, they heard proportionally more adult words during book reading than at any other time. Furthermore, Soderstrom and Wittebolle (2013) found that, during the storytimes recorded in the children's homes, the infants vocalised far more than they did during the storytimes at childcare. The researchers posited that "likely this has to do with storytime being a one-on-one activity at home, while it is typically a large group activity in daycare" (p. 10). Recent neurological research provides further support for the importance of shared reading for children's development, as it suggests that young children's experiences with books and reading contribute directly to their brain development (Hutton et al., 2015).

It is important for infants and toddlers attending ECEC to have the opportunity to participate actively during shared reading, beyond simply listening to the printed words read aloud by educators. As Hoffman and Cassano (2013) explain "Reading with babies and toddlers is distinct from reading aloud with older children, because it requires a highly individualized approach that allows for adult responsiveness to the baby or toddlers' unique needs" (p. 20). Each infant will benefit from the opportunity to see and touch the book, sit on the educator's lap, interact with the educator, flip through the pages, and otherwise play an active role. This suggests a need for educators to provide frequent opportunities for infants to engage with books on a one-to-one basis.

Frequency and Qualities of Shared Reading in ECEC Infant and Toddler Rooms

Studies indicate that shared reading is not a regular practice in many infant and toddler rooms, especially with infants who are younger than twelve months of age (Boardman & Levy, 2019; Holland, 2008; Honig & Shin, 2001; Soundy, 1997). Torr (2019), for example, observed 20 focus infants aged between 10 and 23 months for three hours as they went about their normal activities in their 20 separate ECEC infant rooms. She found that nine of the infants did not participate in any book-focused interactions during that period. Furthermore, all but three of the infants' rooms received a lower ITERS-R (Harms et al., 2006) rating for the indicator "using books", compared with their ratings for "helping children use language" and "helping children understand language".

Torr's (2019) study was part of a larger project focusing on the language environments pertaining in 56 separate ECEC infant rooms in Sydney, Australia. As part of the project, Degotardi et al. (2018) compared the questioning patterns of 27 infant educators, each of whom worked in a different ECEC centre, in two different contexts; shared reading and educator-mediated play. Although not the main focus of Degotardi et al.'s (2018) study, it was noteworthy that only 25 of the 56 educators who participated in this study engaged in 10 or more minutes of shared reading during the three hours of videorecording. Towell et al. (2019) explored the book preferences and book engagement of 12 infants (ages 6–22 months) who attend the same ECEC centre. For 10 weeks, each infant was read to individually once a week by a teacher using a pre-prepared script. Towell et al. (2019) found that infants' engagement with a book tended to be fleeting, as it ranged from 2 minutes 45 seconds to 4 minutes and 20 seconds.

Factors Associated with Shared Reading in ECEC

Given the importance of shared reading as a pedagogical practice in ECEC, and the fact that it is not a regular practice in many ECEC infant and toddler rooms, it is pertinent to consider what factors may facilitate or mitigate against the learning potential of shared reading in these settings. Research suggests that two factors may indirectly influence the educators' talk in general, with implications for their talk during shared reading in particular. First, educators' early childhood qualifications are associated with their use of pedagogical questioning and reasoning talk when interacting with infants and toddlers. Secondly, group size during shared reading affects the educator's ability to respond to, and extend on, individual children's participation during shared reading.

Educators' Early Childhood Qualifications

Children's engagement during shared reading is strongest when educators not only read the picture book aloud but also encourage children's participation by asking questions, responding to their initiations and encouraging turn-taking (Gardner-Neblett et al., 2017). Questioning has long been regarded as an important pedagogical strategy in early childhood educational contexts (Davis & Torr, 2015).

Degotardi et al. (2018) define pedagogical questioning as "educator questions that have an explicitly educational intention, as they are concerned with the construction of knowledge and linguistic representation of experience" (p. 1005). Degotardi et al. (2018) compared the patterns of pedagogical questioning produced by 27 differently qualified early childhood educators during picture book reading and educator-mediated play. Eight educators had a bachelor's degree qualification in early childhood education, and 19 educators had either a diploma or certificate vocational qualification in early childhood education. The study found that educators with different qualifications varied in the ways they used pedagogical questioning in both contexts.

While both groups of educators asked questions to encourage infants to name objects depicted in picture books (*what's that*), bachelor-qualified educators were more likely to extend on the child's utterance by providing additional, decontextualised, information. For example, during one interaction, one infant referred to the picture of a glass of liquid in a picture book by saying "juice". The child's educator extended on the topic of the child's utterance by saying "It does look like juice. It's a special juice called lemonade" (Degotardi et al., 2018, p. 1014). Topic extension is an important strategy in facilitating early language development (Girolametto & Weitzman, 2002).

Example 7.1 presents a more extended example of a degree-qualified educator building on the contributions of toddler Zara during shared reading. This educator used "specify questions" to ask for the name of an object or entity (*what's that; what's inside our flowers*) and "confirm (yes/no) questions" to position Zara as an active participant in a mutually engaging conversation about the meanings in the picture book.

Example 7.1

> [*Zara sits down beside the educator and places a lift-the-flap picture book on the educator's lap.*]

ZARA: Wow, wow.
EDUCATOR: [*lifting a flap*] What is it? Look, it's a mole. He's having a drink. And look! He's got some strawberries. See the strawberries?
ZARA: [*approximating the pronunciation of the word strawberries and pointing to pictures on the page*] Strawberries. Strawberries.
EDUCATOR: Mm. That's an umbrella. Big umbrella to shade you from the sun. Look! He's wearing sunglasses and he's got some books.
ZARA: Oh, oh, oh.
EDUCATOR: Is he watering his garden? [*lifting flap and pausing*] What's inside our flowers? Got daisies. Beautiful. And petunias.
ZARA: [*approximating*] Daisies.

EDUCATOR: And a sunflower. He's gardening. Look what he's growing! That's potatoes. Look how brown they are. They're growing in the soil … in the dirt.

ZARA: [*pointing*] Oranges.

EDUCATOR: That's a pumpkin. It looks a bit like an orange, doesn't it?

[*Educator begins talking to a nearby child who is upset, tries to comfort him, and invites him to join them*] Shall we get Freddy?

ZARA: [*still engrossed in the pictures*] Buckee. Buckee [?*pumpkin*]. Oranges. Oranges.

Example 7.1 was very brief, less than three minutes, but rich in opportunities for language and literacy learning, and for building up Zara's field knowledge about gardening. The educator used semantically related vocabulary (fruit, vegetables, flowers) and drew Zara's attention (look) to the connections between watering and growing plants. She introduced what may have been new words for Zara, by juxtaposing a word Zara is likely to know (dirt) with a more "technical" term (soil). She built on Zara's engagement by asking questions and extending the talk by drawing attention to similarities between oranges and pumpkins. She showed Zara that she valued books and reading by expressing her interest and enjoyment in the activity, and she also pointed out that the mole in the picture was carrying some books. Her whole demeanour was enthusiastic and engaging.

Educators' early childhood qualifications have also been associated with other verbal behaviours that are indirectly related to educators' talk during shared reading. Hu et al. (2019) found that, in the context of using language to direct the behaviour of a child, bachelor qualified early childhood educators were more likely than vocationally qualified educators to provide a reason for their direction. Examples provided by Hu et al. (2019) include reasoning statements such as "it's a bit slippery isn't it …the grass is a bit wet" and "I have to leave and check our oven because I don't want our cookies to get burnt". While Hu et al.'s study did not focus specifically on shared reading, it is feasible that bachelor-qualified educators would also provide infants with the reasons for their imperatives during shared reading, for example "sit down please so your friends can see the pictures too".

Group Size

When reading picture books with infants and toddlers in a group, educators not only need to read the printed text aloud and engage in extra-textual facilitative talk, they also need to manage the group dynamics, so that each child is comfortable, can easily see the book, understands that others also need to see the book, and can hear the talk around the text without straining (Torr, 2020; Wasik, 2008). Studies have identified the particular challenges in reading picture books with children under three years in a group setting. Shared reading with children of this age group is unlike reading with older children, as Harms et al. (2006) point out "it is very challenging to meet the needs of infants and toddlers in a group care setting because each of these very young children requires a great deal of personal attention in order to thrive" (p. 1). The need for individual attention is especially important during shared reading. The larger the group, the greater will be the need for the educator to interrupt the flow of the shared reading to use directive language to manage the children's behaviour (Girolametto et al., 2000; Torr & Pham, 2016), which interrupts the meaning making of the experience and leads to children becoming distracted and disengaged.

Several intervention studies have confirmed that group size affects the qualities of shared reading as a pedagogical activity. In intervention studies, the researchers intervene, or make a change, in a child's environment by manipulating the shared reading situation in some way. They measure children's language before an intervention, using standardised tests for language and other skills, and then intervene by changing the situation in some way, and then measure it again after the intervention. They then compare the control group with the intervention group, and any changes that are identified are assumed to be the result of the intervention. Intervention studies have provided valuable evidence supporting the importance of reading picture books with young children (O'Farrelly et al., 2018).

Phillips and Twardosz (2003), for example, conducted an intervention study with six early childhood educators and fifteen two year old children. The educators were provided with picture books and trained in how to talk to the infants during shared reading, including how to ask questions, prompt for responses, give information and manage the group. The educators were then asked to read to two different groups of children. One group contained eight children and the other contained three children. The children in the smaller group verbalised more and participated physically by touching and handling the picture book, smiling and touching the educator, and making animal noises and other vocalisations.

Other research in various settings has confirmed that, when interacting with two or more young children (rather than an individual child), adults tend to produce more directive talk, and children have less opportunity to participate actively (Girolametto et al., 2000). Cicognani and Zani (1992) compared the speech of two teachers in dyadic (one-to-one) and polyadic (one-to-many) interactions. Ten infants participated in this study, four of whom were aged 10–11 months, and six of whom were aged 31–37 months. Each teacher was tasked with introducing a new toy to an individual child, then separately to a group of three children. The findings revealed that, when interacting with the younger single child, the teachers provided more expressions of approval and encouragement, and gave more explanations. When interacting with the older single child, the teachers additionally produced more exclamations in order to encourage the child's efforts. When interacting with the children in the group situation, however, the teachers produced more imperatives and closed questions. The research suggested that, in the dyadic situation, the teachers were focused on encouraging the infants to verbalise, whereas in the polyadic situation, the teachers were focused more on maintaining the children's attention. This small study demonstrated that the number of infants involved in an interaction affects their language learning opportunities.

Shared Reading as a Context of Situation

Shared reading involves the interaction between different modes of meaning making, including spoken language, written language read aloud, visual images, and non-verbal gestures. Given the complexity of these multiple meaning-making processes, it is useful to be guided by a language-based theory of learning when planning early childhood language and literacy programs. Systemic functional linguistic theory (SFL) posits that three features of the non-linguistic environment (the "material setting" in which an activity occurs) directly and systematically shape the language choices available to speakers within that setting (Halliday & Hasan, 1989). These features of the material setting are referred to as the *field, tenor,* and *mode.* Each of these variables is realised in different parts of the grammar of a language.

The *field* is the social activity that the participants are engaged in; for example, playing a game, baking a cake, eating lunch, or planting sunflower seeds. The field is realised in the *experiential metafunction* of language, which is the function language serves to represent experience, which "enables human beings to build a mental picture of reality, to make sense of what goes on around them and inside them" (Halliday, 1994, p. 106). Speakers represent their experience through their choices of *vocabulary and grammatical structures* (termed "transitivity").

Shared reading of picture books provides many opportunities for educators to facilitate infants' and toddlers' production and comprehension of vocabulary. Picture books introduce children to new and unusual words that are unlikely to be encountered in any other situation. Novel words are introduced in a context which is supported by the illustrations and the guidance of educators. According to SFL theory, when a child learns a new word they are at the same time learning a new concept, idea or gaining new background knowledge. When educators talk about the pictures while observing infants' and toddlers' verbal and non-verbal responses, they can gain important information about the extent of the children's comprehension, and use this information to explain the meanings in the book using different words, non-verbal gestures and facial expressions to achieve shared meaning.

The *tenor* refers to the relationship between the speakers. Tenor is realised in the *interpersonal metafunction* of language, which is the function language serves as an act of communication. Speakers may use language to ask a question (interrogative), make a statement (declarative), issue a command (imperative) or make an offer. Infants and toddlers learn best when educators speak to them using a form of language referred to as "child-addressed speech". This type of speech is positive, responsive to the child's feelings, related to the child's current focus of attention, and encourages turn-taking between educator and child, thus facilitating conversation-like exchanges (Hirsh-Pasek et al., 2015; Topping et al., 2013). Picture books provide the content around which educators can weave conversations with very young children. Simply being exposed to overheard speech in the environment is not sufficient input for children's language development (Golinkoff et al., 2015).

The *mode* is realised in the *textual meta-function* of language, which serves to "knit together" stretches of text to create a cohesive and coherent whole. Shared reading is one of the few activities in ECEC centres that is entirely constituted by language. It thus provides children under three with experiences of decontextualised language, which are essential for future literacy skills and reading development. Shared reading also stimulates pretend play, which is also strongly related to language and literacy development.

Together these three variables – field, tenor, and mode – comprise the *context of situation* of a piece of spoken or written language (referred to as *text*). Each complete sentence or clause simultaneously combines these three strands of meaning – experiential, interpersonal and textual. This means that a change in one of the variables will have implications for the language choices available to the participants during the particular activity. For example, each time a new picture book is read aloud, features of the educator–child talk surrounding the shared reading will also differ in terms of the language learning potential. Repeated readings of a child's favourite picture book will enable a child to notice new details in the pictures and gain new knowledge about the overall meanings (McGee & Schickedanz, 2011), with support from an educator.

Picture books are uniquely equipped to provide language stimulation, as Scott-Mitchell explains:

> Every good picture book contains more than any one person can detect, because it comes from the imagination of the writer or artist and works on many levels – words and pictures independently but also together, what is written and what is illustrated, and, just as importantly, what is left unsaid (the spaces in between) activate the imagination of the individual and can contribute to the growth of the person emotionally, spiritually and intellectually.
>
> (Scott-Mitchell, 1987, p. 76)

As Schickedanz and Collins (2012) point out, however, the illustrations in picture books are far from transparent to very young children. Their careful analysis of young children's misunderstandings of the meanings expressed through visual images reinforces the importance of teachers' talk in facilitating children's learning.

A Snapshot of a Shared Reading Episode in ECEC

Some of the benefits and challenges of shared reading with groups of infants and toddlers can be explored through an analysis of a naturally occurring shared reading experience. Example 7.2 is an extract from a much longer transcription of a shared reading episode between an educator, Kate, a 22 month old focus child

Amy, and three other toddlers attending the same ECEC centre. This centre was rated as "excellent" on the ITERS-R rating scale (Harms et al., 2006).

The educator is reading from a picture book titled *Snail Trail* (Brown, 2000). The illustration of a snail on the cover of the book is presented at the eye level of the viewing child, immediately creating a connection between the viewer and the snail character. The book recounts the journey of the snail as he travels playfully through various landscapes, until the final double-page spread in which the snail is shown sound asleep in a "cave". The viewing perspective on this final page differs from the previous pages, as the viewer is now looking down at the tiny snail from above. A white dotted line (the silvery snail trail) invites the child viewer to retrace the snail's movements, leading to the realisation that the hill, arch, cave, and other landforms that the snail encountered on the trail were in fact, from a human perspective, everyday familiar garden items. The printed text, comprising just 73 words, is clearly separated from the illustrations, thus subtly indicating that speech and print are different ways of making meaning. As the educator Kate reads the printed text aloud to the children, she changes some of the wording slightly. The four listening children are highly engaged in the experience.

Example 7.2

EDUCATOR: [*after settling the toddlers in a small circle around her, so that each one can see the pictures clearly, she begins reading*] There we go. Ready? [*turns to first page*]
"Slimy snail set out on a trail on a bright and sunny morning". There he is! Look. Can you see the sun shining down? [*she traces the slanting diagonal lines representing rays of sunlight with her finger across the page*]
And the snail coming. There's his big shell. [*she uses her finger to trace the circles of the spiral shell*] Goes around and around and around.
It's just like the snails we had, isn't it!
"He went up a hill that was very steep". Up up up up! [*she moves her finger up the page*] "Through a tunnel very gloomy". Ooh, it's a bit dark inside that tunnel. And "into a forest where it was very very quiet".
"Over a bridge very high, down a slope, very very slippery".
Look he's going shuuung! [*she points to the "whoosh" lines depicting the snail's rapid descent*] Oliver, please stop trying to eat your friend's (cards?)
Ooh, look! He's trying to fit though the arch. It's a bit squishy. That space is a bit small.
AMY: There. There.
EDUCATOR: What is it Amy?
OTHER CHILD: Ooh squishy.
EDUCATOR: Yeah. Squishy. He's trying to fit his shell though the archway. Leila, leave her shoes please. Look, here he is, fast asleep.

[*The other children become distracted, but Amy remains focused intently on the last picture of the sleeping snail. Then the other children accidently jostle her, and she looks away from the book and passes a small object, possibly a gumnut, to educator*]

Kate. Kate tries to re-engage Amy. At this stage two of the children move away to other activities but Amy and another child continue looking at the last page of the picture book with educator Kate.]

EDUCATOR: Look, there's the snail and he's fast asleep. And we didn't read this page before. He was soon asleep. Can you see where the snail has been?

Look, there's his silvery snail trail sliding up and down and around over the garden glove, around the pots.

AMY: Where is he?

EDUCATOR: Can you find him in that picture?

AMY: There. [*pointing*]

OTHER CHILD: He's not there.

EDUCATOR: There's the snail's silvery trail [*following the white line with her finger*]. It goes all the way down and over the shovel, down the shovel, through the archways, up into a dark cave. Can you see where he is now?

Lucy, just move back a little bit so that your friends behind you can see. Can you see? There he is Oliver. He's hiding in the cave.

AMY: [*pointing*] There he is. He just a bit sleeping.

EDUCATOR: He's sleeping?

OTHER CHILD: [*unintelligible*] I want to read it again.

EDUCATOR: You want to read it again?

[*settling children*] What else can you see in there Amy? [*Amy flips back through the pages*] Through the archways. [*Amy continues turning the pages*]

Oh! And there he goes into the forest.

OTHER CHILD: No don't! [*she tries to stop Amy turning the pages*]

EDUCATOR: Amy's just turning the pages. I think she'd like to go back this way and see what's at the beginning of the story. [*Amy continues to turn pages, Other child is not pleased, and the two children look at each other warily*]

AMY: [*takes the book off Kate's lap*] No!

EDUCATOR: You're not going to share it anymore? With Lucy?

AMY: No! [*turns away with book*]

EDUCATOR: Okay.

OTHER CHILD: I want to share!

EDUCATOR: Yeah, I'd like to share it. Can you share it with us, Amy? How about this.

Amy can have a look for a little bit then share it with us. [*Amy listens to the plan with the book in her lap, turning pages*]

AMY: [*vocalising to herself*] That. That. Do that. [*Amy finishes turning the pages and leaves the group. Educator Kate stays where she is, and other children come to her, asking for another story*]

Shared Reading and Learning through Language

This shared reading episode is first and foremost an enjoyable and entertaining experience for young children. The children in Example 7.2 have already listened to three repetitions and are keen to listen to the story again. It is also a pedagogical experience providing subtle "lessons" about the meaning-making potential of words and pictures. The learning potential can be understood in terms of the content, subject matter or themes expressed in the picture book, and in the talk surrounding the book (field). There is also the potential for children to use language as a vehicle for interpreting the meanings by asking questions and making comments about the book (tenor). Finally the picture book itself expresses its meanings through different semiotic modes, visual and verbal. A discussion of each variable in Example 7.2 follows.

Field

There are at least three fields being expressed through the language during this shared reading. First, there is the field realised in the words in the picture book text itself. The snail's movement along the trail is expressed through material ("doing") processes (*set out, went, curled up*) and the location is expressed through a series of phrases (*up a hill, into a forest, over a bridge*). The qualities or attributes of each landscape are expressed through a series of relational attributive processes (*it was very steep, gloomy, quiet, high, slippery, narrow*). Many of these words are likely to be new to the infants and toddlers, but they are encountered in a language-rich and visually supportive context through the illustrations and the mediating gestures of the educator, thus facilitating opportunities for learning.

The language in this picture book is unlike the language of everyday speech. There is a highly patterned use of repetition, giving the text a poetic quality. These patterns include repetition of sound through alliteration (*slimy snail*), rhyme (*snail, trail*), rhythm (regular beat) and grammatical structure (prepositional phrases). Despite its apparent simplicity and playfulness, this little book introduces children to a recurrent literary and cultural theme; that a journey can be both physical and metaphorical. Children venture out into the world, but at the end of the journey they return home and fall into a deep sleep (Griffith & Torr, 2003).

Secondly, there is the field construed by the educator through her mediating talk and gestures. From the educator's perspective, this field serves an educational function. She uses gestures to accompany her explanations of how the pictures "mean"; for example by explaining the meaning of the "whoosh" marks that represent the snail's downward slide (*he's going shuuung*) or by tracing the diagonal marks that represent the rays of sunlight with her finger (*can you see the sun shining down*).

The educator provides reasons for her interpretations (*he's trying to fit through the arch; it's a bit squishy; that space is a bit small; he's trying to fit his shell through the archway*), thus making her thinking visible to the children (van Kleeck et al., 1996). She uses different words (*squishy, small*) to present the same or a similar concept to facilitate children's understanding. The educator–child talk about the text serves as a contrast to the literary language of the text itself, thus juxtaposing spoken and written language and providing infants and toddlers with an experience of both modes. Another feature of the educator's talk is her use of unusual vocabulary that is not in the printed text; for example *shovel, archway, silvery.*

Thirdly, there is the field construed in the educator's language as a means of directing the children's behaviour so that the shared reading can proceed smoothly and comfortably and be inclusive of all children. This field is realised in the everyday vocabulary needed to manage a group of young children; for example *leave her shoes please; just move back a little bit so that your friends behind you can see.* It is noticeable that the educator uses politeness expressions, and provides reasons for her directions. Studies show that university-qualified educators are significantly more likely to provide reasons when they direct children's behaviour (Hu et al., 2019), compared with less highly qualified educators. This feature of the field is expressed through the everyday instrumental talk required to get things done in group situations with very young children.

Tenor

There are two types of interpersonal relationship expressed through the talk during this shared reading. First, there is the relationship between the author/illustrator and the reader/viewer of the picture book. The printed text comprises a series of statements of fact, inviting the child viewer to observe, rather than interact with, the snail on his journey. In this respect, the book differs from many well-known picture books which directly engage the child viewer by asking questions, for example *Where is the Green Sheep* (Fox & Horacek, 2004), *How Do I Put It On* (Watanabe & Ohtomo, 1977), and *Have You Seen My Duckling* (Tafuri, 1984).

The tenor also reflects the imbalance of power between the educator and the children. The educator's position of power is expressed linguistically as she asks the questions, provides explanations, and directs the children's behaviour. This provides the children with experiences that foreshadow the types of pedagogical interactions that are associated with school-based learning activities. The child Amy initiates interactions by drawing attention to an element in the picture (*he just a bit sleeping*) and asking a question (*where is he?*). The relationship between Amy and her peers is expressed verbally and through gestures when both children want to have control of the picture book.

Mode

The mode refers to the relationship between the material context and the language choices of the participants. The physical setting during which the shared reading takes place does not feature in the language produced during the shared reading, so it is ancillary to the language choices. The group context does affect the language choices of the participants to the extent that the educator needs to use language to manage the children's behaviour in order for the shared reading to proceed smoothly. This part of the shared reading experience (managing behaviour) is ancillary to the meaning making function of the extra-textual talk surrounding the picture book. The actual reading and talking about the picture books is, however, entirely constituted through the language of the participants as they talk about the meanings expressed through the words and pictures.

To sum up, this brief analysis of one extract of a shared reading episode provides a snapshot of the richness of the meaning making that can occur during this book-focused activity. It is not surprising that abundant research shows that the amount and qualities of shared reading experienced by infants and toddlers is predictive of their future language development and reading achievement at school (Horowitz-Kraus & Hutton, 2015; Shahaeian et al., 2018). Shared reading builds the foundations of future reading because it exposes infants to unusual vocabulary and grammar, builds background knowledge about the world, and provides experience of decontextualised language, within an emotionally supportive environment that is both entertaining and informative.

Noise Levels in Early Childhood Education and Care Centres

Currently there is little empirical evidence to prove that background noise in Early Childhood Education and Care centres has an effect on shared reading of picture books, or even the qualities of the language and literacy environment more generally, although anecdotal reports suggest it is a serious issue. An essential pre-condition for educator-infant conversations to take place is an environment which is quiet enough for each participant to hear the other speaking comfortably, without strain, and not in conflict with background noise. One feature of the language environment pertaining in long day care centres which is rarely discussed in educational linguistic research is the level of background noise to which children and educators are frequently exposed. The term *non-auditory noise* refers to noise levels which are not so elevated as to cause actual hearing impairment, but which nevertheless may impact upon children's health, learning and development. In terms of the quality and safety of the Early Childhood Education and Care centre, Harms et al. (2006) explain that "Constant noise interferes with children's ability to hear language (Ex. Loud music on most of day; much crying throughout the day; inadequate sound absorbing materials in room.)" (p. 30).

Concluding Remarks

Many children aged under three years spend much of their time in Early Childhood Education and Care centres. The experience of shared reading in ECEC centres differs from maternal shared reading in terms of the field, tenor and mode variables, with implications for the language learning environment in general. Educators are in a position to provide plentiful language-rich and nurturing experiences with books and reading, thus providing both education and care to young children. With each shared reading experience, children under three years of age have the opportunity to learn new "ways of knowing" about words, pictures, books and reading, including the following.

- Reading books is enjoyable.
- Books are handled in certain ways.
- Pictures can be talked about.
- Some parts of the pictures are more important than others.
- All books share some features in common.
- All books are different too.
- Books relate to one's own life.

References

Boardman, K., & Levy, R. (2019). "I hadn't realised that whilst the babies and toddlers are sleeping, the other children can't get to the books!": The complexities of "access" to early reading resources for under-threes. *Early Years: An International Research Journal*, 41(5), 443–457. doi:10.1080/09575146.2019.1605336.

Brown, R. (2000). *Snail trail*. Andersen Press.

Cicognani, E., & Zani, B. (1992). Teacher–child interactions in a nursery school: An exploratory study. *Language and Education*, 6(1), 1–12. doi:10.1080/09500789209541321.

Davis, B., & Torr, J. (2015). Educators' use of questioning as a pedagogical strategy in long day care nurseries. *Early Years: An International Research Journal*, 36(1), 1–15. doi:10.1080/09575146.2015.1087974.

Degotardi, S., Torr, J., & Han, F. (2018). Infant educators' use of pedagogical questioning: Relationships with the context of interaction and educators' qualifications. *Early Education and Development*, 29(8), 1004–1018. doi:10.1080/10409289.2018.149900.

Demir-Lira, O. E., Applebaum, L. R., Goldin-Meadow, S., & Levine, S. C. (2019). Parents' early book reading to children: Relation to children's later language and literacy outcomes controlling for other parent language input. *Developmental Science*, 22(3), e12764. doi:10.1111/desc.12764.

Fox, M., & Horacek, J. (2004). *Where is the green sheep?* Puffin.

Gardner-Neblett, N., Holochwost, S. J., Gallagher, K. C., Iruka, I. U., Odom, S. L., & Bruno, E. P. (2017). Books and toddlers in child care: Under what conditions are children most engaged. *Child Youth Care Forum*, 46, 473–493. doi:10.1007/s10566-017-9391-4.

Girolametto, L., & Weitzman, E. (2002). Responsiveness of child care providers in interactions with toddlers and pre-schoolers. *Language, Speech and Hearing in Schools*, 33, 268–281.

Girolametto, L., Weitzman, E., Van Lieshout, R., & Duff, D. (2000) Directiveness in teachers' language input to toddlers and pre-schoolers in day care. *Journal of Speech, Language and Hearing Research*, 43, 1101–1114. doi:10.1044/jslhr.4305.1101.

Golinkoff, R. M., Can, D. D., Soderstrom, M., & Hirsh-Pasek, K. (2015). (Baby) talk to me: The social context of infant-directed speech and its effects on early language acquisition. *Current Directions in Psychological Science*, 24(5), 339–344. www.jstor.org/stable/44318893

Griffith, K., & Torr, J. (2003). Playfulness in children's books about bedtime: Ambivalence and subversion in the bedtime story. *Papers: Explorations into Children's Literature*, 13(1), 11–24.

Halliday, M. A. K. (1994). *An introduction to functional grammar* (2nd ed.). Edward Arnold.

Halliday, M. A. K., & Hasan, R. (1989). *Language, context and text: Aspects of language in a social-semiotic perspective* (2nd ed.). Oxford University Press.

Harms, T., Cryer, D., & Clifford, R. M. (2006). *Infant/Toddler Environment Rating Scale – Revised* (ITERS-R). Teachers College Press.

Harms, T., Cryer, D., Clifford, R. M., & Yazejian, N. (2017). *Infant/Toddler Environment Rating Scale* (ITERS-3) (3rd ed.). Teachers College Press.

Hirsh-Pasek, K., Adamson, L. G., Bakeman, R., Owen, M. T., Golinkoff, R. M., Pace, A., Yust, P. K. S., & Suma, K. (2015). The contribution of early communication quality to low-income children's language success. *Psychological Science*, 26(7), 1071–1083. doi:10.1177/0956797615581493.

Hoffman, J. L., & Cassano, C. (2013). The beginning: Reading with babies and toddlers. In J. A. Schickedanz & M. F. Collins (Eds.), *So much more than the ABCs* (pp. 19–40). National Association for the Education of Young Children.

Holland, J. W. (2008). Reading aloud with infants: The controversy, the myth, and a case study. *Early Childhood Education Journal*, 35, 383–385.doi:10.1007/s10643-007-0203-6.

Honig, A. S., & Shin, M. (2001). Reading aloud with infants and toddlers in child care settings: An observational study. *Early Childhood Education Journal* 28(3): 193–197. doi:1082-3301/01/0300-0193.

Horowitz-Kraus, T., & Hutton, J. S. (2015). From emergent literacy to reading: How learning to read changes a child's brain. *Acta Paediatrica*, 2015, 104(7), 648–656. doi:10.1111/apa.13018.

Hu, J., Torr, J., Degotardi, S., & Han, F. (2019). Educators' use of commanding language to direct infants' behaviour: Relationship to educators' qualifications and implications for language learning opportunities. *Early Years*, 39(2), 190–204. doi:10.1080/09575146.2017.1368008.

Hu, J., Degotardi, S., Torr, J., & Han, F. (2019). Reasoning as a pedagogical strategy in infant-addressed talk in early childhood education centres: Relationships with educators' qualifications and communicative function. *Early Education and Development*, 30(7), 872–886. doi:10.1080/10409289.2019.1607449.

Hutton, J. S., Horowitz-Kraus, T., Mendelsohn, A. L., DeWitt, T., Holland, S. K. (2015). Home reading environment and brain activation in preschool children listening to stories. *Pediatrics*, 136(3), 466–478. doi:10.1542/peds.2015-0359.

McGee, L. M., & Schickedanz, J. A. (2011). Repeated interactive read-alouds in preschool and kindergarten. *The Reading Teacher*, 60(8), 742–751. doi:10.1598/RT.60.8.4.

NICHD ECCRN. (2000). The relation of child care to cognitive and language development. *Child Development*, 71(4), 960–980. doi:10.1111/1467-8624.00202.

OECD. (2017) *Starting strong 2017: Key OECD indicators one early childhood education and care*. OECD Publishing. doi:10.1787/9787/9789264276116-en.

O'Farrelly, C., Doyle, O., Victory, G., & Palamaro-Munsell, E. (2018) Shared reading in infancy and later development: Evidence from an early intervention. *Journal of Applied Developmental Psychology* 54, 69–83. doi:10.1016/j.appdev.2017.12.001.

Phillips, L. B., & Twardosz, S. (2003). Group size and storybook reading: Two-year-old children's verbal and nonverbal participation with books. *Early Education and Development*, 14(4), 453–478.

Rudd, L. C., Cain, D. W., & Saxon, T. F. (2008). Does improving joint attention in low- quality child-care enhance langauge development? *Early Child Development and Care*, 178(3), 315–338. doi:10.1080/03004430701536582.

Schickedanz, J. A., & Collins, M. F. (2012). For young children, pictures in storybooks are rarely worth a thousand words. *The Reading Teacher*, 65(8), 539–554 doi:10.1002/TRTR.01080.

Scott-Mitchell, C. (1987). Further flight: The picture book. In M. Saxby & G. Winch (Eds.), *Give them wings: The experience of children's literature* (pp.75–90) Macmillan Education Australia.

Shahaeian, A. M., Wang, C., Tucker-Drob, E., Geiger, V., Bus, A. G., & Harrison, L. J. (2018). Early shared reading, socio-economic status, and children's cognitive and school competencies: Six years of longitudinal evidence. *Scientific Studies of Reading*, 22(6), 485–502. doi:10.1080/10888438.2018.1482901.

Soderstrom, M., & Wittebolle, K. (2013). When do caregivers talk? The influences of activity and time of day on caregiver speech and child vocalizations in two childcare environments. *Plos One*. doi:10.1371/journal.pone.0080646.

Soundy, C. S. (1997). Nurturing literacy with infants and toddlers in group settings. *Childhood Education*, 73(3), 149–153. doi:10.1080/00094056.1997.10522673.

Tafuri, N. (1984). *Have you seen my duckling?* William Morrow.

Topping, K., Dekhinet, R., & Zeedyk, S. (2013). Parent-infant interaction and children's language development. *Educational Psychology*, 33(4), 391–415. doi:10.1080/01443410.2012.744159.

Torr, J. (2019). Infants' experiences of shared reading with their educators in Early Childhood Education and Care centres: An observational study. *Early Childhood Education Journal*, 47(5), 519–529. doi:10.1007/s10643-019-00948-2.

Torr, J. (2020). How "shared" is shared reading: Book-focused infant-educator interactions in long daycare centres. *Journal of Early Childhood Literacy*, 20(4), 815–838. doi:10.1177/1468798418792038.

Torr, J., & Pham, L. (2016). Educator talk in long day care nurseries: How context shapes meaning. *Early Childhood Education Journal*, 44, 245–254. doi:10.1007/s10643-015-0705-6.

Towell, J. L., Bartram, L. Morrow, S., & Brown, S. L. (2019). Reading to babies: Exploring the beginnings of literacy. *Journal of Early Childhood*, 21(3), 321–337. doi:10.1177%2F1468798419846199.

van Kleeck, A., Alexander, E. I., Vigil, A., & Templeton, K. E. (1996). Verbally modelling thinking for infants: Middle-class mothers' presentation of information structures during book sharing. *Journal of Research in Childhood Education*, 10(2), 101–113. doi:10.1080/02568549609594893.

Wasik, B. (2008). When fewer is more: Small groups in Early Childhood Classrooms. *Early Childhood Education Journal*, 35, 515–521. doi:10.1007/s10643-008-0245-4.

Watanabe, S., & Ohtomo, Y. (1977). *How do I put it on?* Puffin.

Weisleder, A., & Fernald, A. (2013). Talking to children matters: Early language experience strengthens processing and builds vocabulary. *Psychological Science*, 24, 2143–2152. doi:10.1177/0956797613488145.

Zimmerman, F. J., Gilkerson, J., Richards, J. A., Christakis, D. A., Dongxin, X., Gray, S., & Yapanel, U. (2009). Teaching by listening: The importance of adult–child conversations to langauge development. *Pediatrics*, 124(1), 342–349. doi:10.1542/peds.2008-2267.

8 Picture Books for Children from Birth to Three

Picture books for infants and toddlers have received less critical attention than books intended for older children, but in light of their important role in children's development during the crucial first years of life, it is worth giving them serious attention for several reasons. First, the thematic content of many picture books for this age group stimulates them intellectually and emotionally, thus strengthening children's intrinsic motivation to engage more frequently with books and reading. Secondly, picture books provide children under three with pleasurable experiences of fine artwork and literary language including rhyme, rhythm, and alliteration, which appeal to their senses and foster their aesthetic awareness and emerging literary consciousness. Thirdly, the visual and verbal features of the picture book shape the adult–child interactions surrounding the picture book. This means that the picture book influences the learning potential and construction of knowledge that occurs during shared reading. Given these potential benefits, it is not surprising that there is a strong association between early shared reading and children's intrinsic motivation to learn to read after they commence school (Shahaeian et al., 2018).

Picture Books as Material Objects

Picture books for infants and toddlers come in many shapes and forms. The boundary between a book and a toy is often blurred for very young children (Apseloff, 1987). Unlike picture books for older children, board-books are often packaged with a soft toy to represent the main character in the picture book, such as a plush possum toy with *Possum Magic* (Fox & Vivas, 2004 [1983]) or a caterpillar puppet with *The Very Hungry Caterpillar* (Carle, 1969). These toys serve as a bridge between the two-dimensional visual representation of a character in a picture book, and its three-dimensional counterpart as a toy that can be cuddled and played with.

Picture books for this age group are made of stiff cardboard that can be held, chewed, sucked, and easily wiped clean after use. Some picture books are waterproof and can be played with in the bath along with other bath toys. Board-books are easy to prop open so that pre-mobile infants can gaze at the pictures during "tummy time" on the floor. Elements such as the size, shape

DOI: 10.4324/9781003168812-8

and tactility, and interactive features such as lift-the-flaps and noise-making buttons, invite exploration and build suspense. Characters in popular children's television programs and movies are often presented in a scaled-down board-book format targeted at infants and toddlers, so that the book functions as a marketing tool along with other consumables such as lunchboxes, backpacks and hats (Dunn, 2002; Nodelman & Reimer, 2003). Rarely do such books compare in quality with authentic picture books created by highly gifted authors and illustrators.

Picture Books as Semiotic Texts

Nodelman and Reimer (2003) describe picture books as "short books that tell stories or convey information with relatively few words but pictures on every page" (p. 275). Much of the meaning-making in picture books for very young children occurs through the illustrations, although the printed text also plays an important role. Picture books are complex because they make meaning through the *interaction* between these two different semiotic systems: language and visual images. Each illustration in a picture book has meaning in relation to the other illustrations and the printed text in the picture book in its entirety.

There are three ways in which the illustrations and printed text interact with each other on each page, and from one page to the next, to create the overall meanings realised in the picture book (Lewis, 2001; Nikolajeva & Scott, 2000; Nodelman & Reimer, 2003). First, the illustrations and printed text may *confirm* each other in a relatively straightforward manner. In *The Toolbox* (Rockwell & Rockwell, 1971), for example, the child narrator names each object in his father's toolbox, one by one. Each page contains a beautifully wrought and technically accurate painting of a tool or related object (tape measure, gloves, sandpaper) set against a plain white background. The printed text in large font names each tool and its function; "there are sharp wire cutters and a roll of wire" and "there is sandpaper to smooth wood and plaster". In its simplicity, this picture book uses both visual images and printed text to represent a young child's experience of the world and to communicate that experience to the actual child and adult reading and talking about the picture book together. The child's fascination with the father's well-organised toolbox reflects the child's sense of security and trust in his father.

Secondly, the illustrations in a picture book may *extend* on the meanings expressed in the printed text. In some picture books, the illustrations provide essential information needed for the reader to appreciate fully the meaning of the printed text. In *Rosie's Walk* (Hutchins, 2009 [1967]), for example, two perspectives on the same activity are represented, one in the printed text and one in the illustrations. The printed text presents the world as understood by Rosie, a hen, as she goes for an uneventful walk through the farmyard. The illustrations reveal another perspective, that of a fox who is stalking Rosie. The fox's pursuit is thwarted, however, as he suffers a series of mishaps and accidents, while Rosie remains blissfully oblivious to the danger she is in. This picture book allows the child to become the reader outside the text, looking on and knowing things about the characters that they (the characters) do not know.

The illustrations in picture books extend on the printed text by revealing important details about the setting, time, place, characters and events that are not explicitly referred to in the printed text. In *Old Pig* (Wild & Brooks 1995), for example, the illustrations depict the changing of the seasons, which serve as a metaphor for the passing of time and the impending death of the beloved old pig. Illustrations are relatively open-ended and they allow infants and toddlers to construe their meanings according to their current interests, capabilities and life experiences, and filter out the rest. As Scott-Mitchell (1987) explains "Every good picture book contains more than any one person can detect" (p. 76).

Thirdly, the illustrations in picture books may *contradict* what the written text says, creating ironic and humorous effects. This type of interaction is unlikely to appear in picture books intended for young children under school age. Older children who have had plentiful experiences with books and reading during their preschool years are able to appreciate "metafictional" picture books, as they are already well versed in how picture books typically work, and so can enjoy the subversive ways that metafictional picture books play with traditional content and structure.

The Dual Audience of Picture Books

Picture books for infants and toddlers are written, illustrated, published, critiqued, selected, purchased and read aloud by parents, educators and other caregivers. Therefore any appraisal of picture books for young children must consider their qualities in relation to both the adult reader and the young child listener and viewer. The experience of shared reading from the perspective of a child under three years of age involves looking at the illustrations while simultaneously listening to the printed text read aloud, which is perceived by a preverbal child as an unbroken stream of speech. Even picture books for infants and toddlers can address aspects of the human condition that can only be fully appreciated by an adult reader. Features such as double meanings, intertextual allusions, and visual references to past events, are often addressed to adult readers of picture books for infants and toddlers. When picture books address both the reading adult and the young child, the adult's interest and pleasure during shared reading communicates itself to the child in powerful ways, with implications for future success in reading. As Meek (1982) points out "To learn to read, children need the attention of one patient adult, or older child, for long enough to read something they *both* enjoy" (p. 9; my italics).

As parents and educators read and talk about picture books, they may remember and reflect on those that entertained and stimulated them when they were young (Mangan, 2018; Spufford, 2002). Highly skilled author/illustrators are able to express meanings that appeal to very young children, and are understood by them at face value, while simultaneously appealing to parents and educators who can appreciate them at a deeper level. The picture book *I want my hat back* by an award-winning author/illustrator (Klassen, 2011) can be understood at two levels. It can be enjoyed by a child aged under three as a tale about a bear who lost his hat, an experience shared by many young children. The story ends with the bear finding his hat, but the adult reader will detect a darker meaning that is not understood by young viewers and listeners.

The Baby's Catalogue (Ahlberg & Ahlberg, 1982) is an example of a picture book that clearly addresses a dual readership. This picture book presents a day in the life of six babies and their families, from when the babies wake in the morning until they go to sleep in the evening. The intersecting lives of each family member (baby, mother, father, sibling, pet) are represented on each page, with a topic heading; for example, "Mornings", "High Chairs and Breakfasts", "Nappies and Games", "Baths and Bedtimes". The different behaviours of each family member under each "topic" heading depict experiences that an actual child and adult can relate to in their own lives. The illustrations under the heading "accidents" gently and humorously reveal that what is an accident for one person may not be perceived as an accident by another.

One approach to understanding the dual readership of picture books for infants and toddlers is to invoke the concept of an "implied reader" (Cocks, 2004). As Rosenblatt (1982) theorised, for adult readers "reading is a transaction, a two-way process, involving a reader and a text at a particular time under particular circumstances" (p. 268). Chambers (1985) explains that authors of literary texts reveal their values and attitudes indirectly, and in doing so "construct" a particular type of reader inscribed in the text itself, one who will appreciate the language, style, content, theme, and attitudes expressed in the text. This concept of an implied reader has proven relevant in understanding the dual perspectives of adults and children in relation to what is ostensibly the "same" picture book text.

The actual child and adult reading and talking about a picture book in the present moment are not necessarily the same as the adult and child implied in the picture book itself. Nodelman & Reimer (2003) refer to the dual readership as comprising a "double implied reader" (p. 21). How an infant or toddler responds to a picture book will depend on multiple factors including the child's previous experiences with pictures and picture books, their language growth, physical capabilities, background knowledge, familiarity with the adult reader, curiosity about the topic, and the presence of other children.

During shared reading, the gap between the implied child reader and the actual child reader is mediated through the guidance and explanations of the adult reader. The wider the gap between implied and actual child viewers, the more necessary is the adult's role as a guide and facilitator of the child's understanding during shared reading. This gap between the implied and the actual reader/viewer is very evident in the award-winning picture book *Peepo!* (Ahlberg & Ahlberg, 1983). The recto side of each double page has a peephole cut in it. The actual child reader/viewer is invited to look through this peephole and see the world from the baby's perspective; "here's a little baby, 1 2 3, stands in his cot, what does he see". The view through each page's peephole reveals a different member of the baby's family (mother, father, grandmother, siblings). Each turn of the page refocuses the peephole so that it provides a frame for the baby himself, safe and secure in his warm and nurturing environment. For contemporary infants and toddlers, this picture book is likely to resonate with the turn-taking games and nursery rhymes that they themselves have engaged in with parents and caregivers. The poetic language of the written text captures and retains the attention of the very young, because they have been immersed in such language from birth.

Adult readers, however, are likely to recognise the deeper meanings presented through the illustrations. Although never referred to directly in the printed text, the illustrations reveal that the family is living in a London street during World War II. Each illustration subtly includes evidence that the family is facing an existential threat: a bombed out building near the park, a picture of Churchill on the wall of the sitting room, the father wearing his army uniform. These details juxtapose the baby's perception of the world as a secure and comfortable place with an adult's awareness that the wider world can be dangerous and frightening. During shared reading of this picture book, the actual adult reader/viewer is likely to focus on the playful aspects only (as do the parents and grandmother represented in the picture book itself who are either calm or smiling), while being privately moved as they reflect on the circumstances under which the family is living.

The juxtaposition of adult and child perspectives on what is ostensibly the "same" picture book is an important indicator of quality in children's literature. Author/illustrators of successful picture books for children under three years recognise that they are addressing a dual audience and must appeal to both adult and child readers and viewers. The child narrator in *The Blanket* (Burningham, 1975) addresses the child viewer by recounting his troubling realisation at bedtime that his security blanket is missing. Burningham (1975) also addresses the actual parents who are reading this picture book to their own child. The illustrations reflect how parents typically react to such a frustrating situation, as (tired and in need of a break) they recognise that without his security blanket the child is unlikely to be able to settle to sleep. The child narrator's straightforward statements of fact (*Mummy looked in the bathroom … Daddy looked in the cupboard*) belie the depicted feelings of the parents in the book, as they search for the missing blanket, and resonate with the actual parents who are reading this book to their own child.

The Illustrations in Picture Books for Infants and Toddlers

The illustrations in picture books for infants and toddlers include a wide diversity of artistic styles, including naturalism, realism, surrealism and impressionism. They use a range of media, ranging from watercolour, oils, block print, pastels, charcoals, black and white ink drawings, collage and many others. The pictures in picture books are rarely representational in the same way that photographs are. As Nodelman (1996) points out "Even representational pictures – the ones we call realistic – exist within systems of learned codes, and thus make little sense to anyone without a previous knowledge of those systems" (p. 217). As Golden and Gerber (1990) explain, pictures are about ideas and concepts, not objects. Some of the most esteemed picture books for infants and toddlers contain pictures that are entirely fantastical; for example gruffalos, green sheep, animals wearing clothes, and so on.

Children and adults respond to pictures aesthetically and emotionally, as they gain pleasure from the patterns and colours in works of art, including those in picture books (Kiefer, 1988). Infants enjoy looking at pictures and demonstrate their preference for one picture over another by gazing at it, smiling, moving their limbs, and trying to touch it. The pictures in picture books are always more prominent than the printed text, and wordless picture books convey their meanings entirely through the pictures; for example in *Sunshine* (Ormerod, 2022a [1982]) and *Moonshine* (Ormerod, 2022b [1982]). Studies show that infants' and toddlers' eyes move around a picture as they gaze at it, and the depicted characters in the illustrations are usually presented at the eye level of the child viewer, creating a feeling of closeness and identification.

The printed letters (graphemes) are an important visual element in picture books, especially those for very young children. The colour, size, placement and qualities of the print contribute aesthetically to the overall presentation of the picture book and add to the meaning as a whole. Some picture books make a clear distinction between the illustrations and the printed text, by consistently presenting the print on one side of each double page spread, and the illustration on the opposite side, as in *The Baby* (Burningham, 1974) and *Where the Wild Things Are* (Sendak, 1963). The fact that the print is separated from the illustration makes visually explicit the fact that words and pictures create meaning in different but complementary ways.

As Meek (1988) has pointed out, the illustrations in picture books provide children with subtle "lessons" about how to read a picture book. The characters in picture books tend to walk across the page from left to right, as in *Brown Bear Brown Bear What Do You See?* (Carle & Martin, 1997), *Rosie's Walk* (Hutchins, 2009 [1967]), *I Went Walking* (Machin & Vivas, 2014 [1989]), and *Hairy Maclary from Donaldson's Dairy* (Dodd, 2002 [1985]), inviting children to turn the page. The last page will often break this pattern by presenting the character looking directly at the reader, or by showing the character asleep, thus signally "the end".

The Written Language in Picture Books for Infants and Toddlers

The illustrations and written text in picture books serve different functions. In picture books for infants and toddlers there is minimal written text, because much of the meaning is expressed visually through the illustrations. The illustrations in the award winning *Roadworks* (Sutton & Lovelock, 2008) convey factual information about the processes involved in making a road, from the initial planning, marking out the site, the use of different types of heavy equipment, to the completion of the road on the final page. The linguistic patterning of the written text, however, resembles the poetic qualities of nursery rhymes, lullabies and turn-taking games. The written language on each double page spread in *Roadworks* is presented in the form of rhyming stanzas, containing repetition, alliteration, assonance, and onomatopoeia; for example "raise the signs, raise the signs, drag and hoist and ram, force them down into their hole, thwack! Whop! Wham!" (Sutton & Lovelock, 2008, np). These literary patterns resonate with children's previous experiences with oral rhymes, and invite them to enjoy the language for its aesthetic qualities, while also inviting them to respond physically and to chime in with the repeated lines.

In her analysis of nursery rhymes, Hasan (1985) identified repetition across linguistic strata as the underlying patterning of this type of literary language. At the phonological level, there is repetition of sound patterns in rhyme, alliteration and assonance. At the grammatical level, there is repetition of the speech functions of question and statement. In *How Do I Put it On?* (Watanabe & Ohtomo, 1978), the bear character puts each item of clothing on incorrectly, for example he puts his underpants on his head, and his cap on his foot. As he does so, the bear speaks directly to the child viewer: "do I put it on like this?" The child can enjoy the humour and, on turning the page, find the response: "No I put my cap on my head". Similarly, in *Are You There, Bear?* (Maris, 1984) the child viewer/listener is exposed to the grammatical patterns of question and response. This grammatical repetition invites the child's engagement through responding to the questions posed in the text.

The written language in picture books is experienced aurally by infants and toddlers as it is read aloud. This means that the adult reader's voice quality, tone, intonation, loudness, facial expressions, gestures and other paralinguistic features all contribute to the overall construction of meaning. In addition to presenting written language read aloud, picture books contain vocabulary which children are unlikely to encounter in any other context (Cameron-Faulkner & Noble, 2013; Montag et al., 2015). In *Roadworks* (Sutton & Lovelock, 2008), for example, there are many words that are specific to the field of road construction, such as *groundwork, roadbed, tar, hoist, ram,* and *lug*. The final page, titled "machine facts", uses technical language accompanied by an illustration to name and describe the function of the different types of earth-moving equipment referred to in the main text. In this way, the book juxtaposes different modes of represented experience: narrative and informational.

Picture books offer rich opportunities for exposing infants and toddlers to technical language in diverse fields, as they bring into the immediate context of situation information about entities that can only be construed through language and pictures, such as dinosaurs, the solar system and so on. Even when the written text does not include technical vocabulary, parents and educators are likely to introduce it verbally during shared reading (Torr & Scott, 2006). Through repeated readings, children become familiar with new and unusual words, and the pictures support their comprehension of the meanings of words in context.

The printed text in picture books for young children exposes them to unusual grammatical structures that they are unlikely to encounter in other contexts. Cameron-Faulkner and Noble (2013) analysed the written texts of 20 picture books marketed as appropriate for two year old children. They found that the picture book texts contained significantly more complex utterances, such as projecting clause complexes (*I know you like jigsaws*) and reported speech ("*amazing" said the mouse*) than did the talk mothers addressed to their child in any other context. Similarly, Montag (2019) analysed a corpus of 100 picture books selected from best-seller lists and based on librarians' recommendations. Montag (2019) compared the frequency of passive constructions ("the milk has already been poured" p. 530) and different types of relative clauses ("here's the kitty who likes that toy" p. 530). She found a greater proportion of these complex constructions in picture books compared with those in mothers' talk with their infant aged from 5–37 months.

Many picture books for infants and toddlers draw on the patterned literary language of nursery rhymes and other oral narrative modes of storytelling. For example, picture books such as *Moo Baa Laa Laa*, (Boynton, 2011 [1984]) and *The Very Hungry Caterpillar* (Carle, 1969) have a musical quality which parents and educators and children enjoy. The linguistic patterning of such texts assist young children to remember some of the words and chime in during the shared reading. In her analysis of the language of nursery rhymes, Hasan (1985) explains that their linguistic patterning provides young children with opportunities to enjoy the aesthetic qualities of such literary language by participating in their recitation: "the development of verbal aesthetics is a specific aspect of the growth of a child's language, and requires participation in a particular kind of discourse" (p. 28).

Ways of Knowing: Narrative and Informational Picture Books

The term register refers to the distinctive linguistic patterns associated with different types of text that serve a particular function in the lives of speakers (Halliday & Hasan, 1989). Picture books for infants and toddlers can be broadly categorised according to whether they are primarily narrative or primarily informational in their form and content. These two registers represent experience and construct knowledge in different ways that complement each other. Bruner (1986) explains that there are "two modes of cognitive functioning, two modes of thought, each providing distinctive ways of ordering experience, of constructing reality" (p. 11).

Narrative Picture Books

One way of representing experience and building knowledge in picture books is to present it in the form of a narrative. Narratives are fictional accounts of events that typically unfold in the past. They express meaning by focusing on the thoughts, feelings, and actions of one or more characters in a particular setting and point in time.

At its most basic, a narrative can be described as having at least four essential structural elements: an orientation, a complication, a crisis, and a resolution. The orientation introduces the reader/viewer to the current situation, setting, and characters. A complication occurs that disrupts the normal pattern of life and presents the main character with a dilemma or problem that has to be solved. The turning point of the tale occurs when a crisis is reached and things must change. Through courage and diligence, the main character resolves the problem and returns to normal life, a little older and a little wiser. These structural elements of narratives make them recognisable to members of a community as "stories" (Bettelheim, 1976; Campbell, 1949). Many nursery rhymes are highly condensed versions of this basic narrative structure (see Examples 8.1 and 8.2). Children's earliest experiences of the narrative register are in often in the form of traditional tales and nursery rhymes.

Example 8.1

ORIENTATION: Jack and Jill went up the hill to fetch a pail of water
COMPLICATION/CRISIS: Jack fell down and broke his crown and Jill came
    tumbling after.
RESOLUTION: Up Jack got and home did trot as fast as he could caper
    He went to bed to mend his head with vinegar and brown paper.

Example 8.2

ORIENTATION: Humpty Dumpty sat on a wall.
COMPLICATION/CRISIS: Humpty Dumpty had a great fall.
RESOLUTION: All the king's horses and all the king's men
    Couldn't put Humpty together again.

While narrative picture books for infants and toddlers conform to this narrative structural pattern, they do so in a way that is relevant to children's life experiences and knowledge about the world. The crisis, for example, may be concerned with a lost toy or the arrival of a new baby. In *The Very Hungry Caterpillar* (Carle, 1969), for example, the orientation introduces the reader/viewer to the tiny egg on its leaf. This is followed by the complication, resulting from the caterpillar's overconsumption of food. The crisis occurs when the caterpillar becomes sick from overeating. The resolution occurs when the caterpillar's health is restored and he becomes a butterfly.

Informational Picture Books

Informational picture books, on the other hand, construct reality in terms of conceptual classes or domains. They represent experience and build knowledge by using the timeless present tense to make generalisations about phenomena. Informational texts are organised according to themes or topics. *My Little Book of Animals* (de la Bedoyere, 2014), for example, organises animals according to where they live, for example grassland, ocean, forest and desert. Each animal is described as one member of a class (*lions are big cats; they live in groups, called prides*). The *Book of Animals* (Martin et al., 2000) explains that while all animals belong to a class (animal) they can be further categorised according to different sets of criteria, such as how they move, the types of skin they have, the noises they make, and so on. When infants and toddlers are exposed to informational books such as this one, they are introduced to the notion of classification and taxonomies as a way of organising knowledge.

The Integration of Narrative and Informational Elements in Picture Books

In the majority of picture books for infants and toddlers, both narrative and informational elements co-exist within the one text, creating a form of "hybrid" text (van Lierop-Debrauwer, 2017). Author/illustrators of picture books playfully manipulate narrative and structural elements in highly imaginative ways. In *Our granny* (Wild & Vivas, 1994), for example, the linguistic patterns typical of the informational register are deployed in a series of generalisations about grandmothers. The child narrator compares and contrasts grandmothers according to their living arrangements, appearance, clothing, and occupations. Despite their individual differences, in the eyes of the child narrator these women all belong to the class "grandmothers".

Nonsense, which involves many elements of language play, is a significant feature of most children's picture books. According to Torr and Griffith (2003) there is no straightforward definition as to what constitutes "nonsense" elements in children's literature, but typical techniques include playing with sound patterns and shapes, depicting the opposites of conventional behaviours, changing the size and shape of animals, portraying animals behaving like humans, putting everyday things in bizarre contexts, and verbal play (Anderson & Apseloff, 1989).

Alphabet Books

Alphabet books are one of the oldest and most popular forms of picture book for children. Originally intended to teach children the alphabet, they no longer explicitly serve that purpose, but rather serve primarily to entertain young children and engage their imaginations. Author/illustrators of alphabet books are constrained by the fixed and unalterable sequence of the 26 letters of the alphabet (Torr & Griffith, 2003) and the requirement that each letter must be accompanied by a pictured entity that starts with its corresponding speech sound.

Within this frame, however, there is ample scope for author/illustrators to produce ABC books that are examples of fine works of art. As Griffith and Torr (2003) explain "The freedom of interpretation and imaginative response lies in the choice of which entities or processes are chosen to depict each letter, how to visually represent them, and the qualities of the accompanying written text, if there is one" (p. 9). Many ABC books integrate both factual and narrative elements in highly imaginative and artistic ways. This can be seen in *Alphabet Book* (Burningham, 1985), which creates cohesion across the 26 letters of the alphabet by the recurring image of a young child who engages with the very objects that are depicted to represent each letter. As found by Torr and Griffith (2003), "What has emerged as paramount in determining how these texts work as literature is, first, the logic of connection which adheres between image and written text, and, secondly, the playful manipulation of this connection through visual and verbal 'nonsense'" (p. 9).

Nursery Rhyme Anthologies

Nursery rhyme anthologies have a unique role to play in children's emergent literacy and aesthetic development. They provide a pathway from oral literature to picture books, confirming the principle that learning occurs during the transition from given to new. While the words of a nursery rhyme may be familiar to a young child, the illustrations will inevitably present new and individualistic interpretations of the strange and nonsensical meanings expressed in nursery rhymes. As with ABC books, illustrators of nursery rhymes are required to reproduce the actual words of the well-known rhymes, but their imaginative response lies in the ways they interpret the meaning visually. Each illustrator of an anthology will interpret the familiar rhymes in new ways.

Thematic Content in Picture Books for Children from Birth to Three

In addition to providing infants and toddlers with enjoyment and language learning opportunities, picture books also have thematic content; that is, they represent experience through their choice of subject matter and the stance they take towards that subject matter. As discussed previously, picture books have a readership comprising both adults and young children, so the cultural attitudes, beliefs and values of a community are likely to be presented in literature for children within that community (Stephens, 1992).

Psychological approaches to children's literature have revealed the powerful effects that picture books and other forms of literature have on young children's psychological, emotional and spiritual growth (Bettelheim, 1976; Reese & Riordan, 2017; Spitz, 1999). Serious themes are often presented through animal characters because they allow children to respond emotionally to the extent that they feel comfortable. Picture books assist children to deal with their concerns by showing them how others have dealt with the same issues and by suggesting solutions. More generally, children come to understand that picture books are relevant to their own lives. They create an opportunity for children to develop empathy, by seeing how children and animals in picture books feel and behave and recognising them in their own lives (Torr, 2007). In her study of the stories created by pre-literate children, Fox (1993) found that all the young children in her study drew on stories which their parents had read to them many times, and that the stories which appeared most in children's own invented narratives were "ones which deal with major fears and strong emotions" (p. 21).

Two themes or motifs recur in highly regarded literature for infants and toddlers.

The Transformative Effects of the Journey

A recurring theme in narratives for infants and toddlers is that of the journey. Just as life is seen as a journey in literary and religious texts for adults, so too the young characters (animal or human) depicted in picture books are shown undertaking a journey of some kind, during which an event occurs that leads the child to new awareness and understanding. In *Snap Went Chester* (Cox & Miller, 2003), Chester the crocodile amuses himself one afternoon by snapping at some of the animals with whom he shares the waters of the Nile River. After successfully chasing away a fly, a painted reed frog, a wild duck, a mongoose, a lion cub, a flamingo and a chimpanzee, he gets his comeuppance when he attempts to snap at a large pelican. This time the tables are turned and the pelican snaps back. Chester, chastened and abashed, returns home to his mother as quickly as he can and spends the rest of the day perched quietly on his mother's head.

The journey as represented in picture books for young children is a literal journey but it also suggests a journey towards growth and independence. The dangers of becoming separated from mother are also a common theme in many picture books for infants and toddlers. In *Come on Daisy* (Simmons, 1988), Daisy's mother warns Daisy to "stay close", but Daisy wanders off to play on the lilypads, chase the dragonflies, watch the fish, and do other interesting things. Her games are interrupted by the screech of a large bird of prey. Daisy is frightened and looks for her mother, and initially cannot find her. The story ends happily when Daisy's mother finds her child. From then on, having learnt her lesson about the dangers lurking in the external world, Daisy always stays close to her mother.

Stories for young children in all cultures convey important messages about how to live a good life. Bettelheim sums up the messages in stories and picture books for young children in this way: "In order not to be at the mercy of the vagaries of life, one must develop one's inner resources, so that one's emotions, imagination, and intellect mutually support and enrich one another" (Bettelheim, 1976, p. 4).

Ambivalence about Bedtime

There is a plethora of picture books about bedtime for infants and toddlers, raising questions as to why this particular moment in the day is so emotionally charged for both parents and infants. According to Griffith and Torr (2003)

"Bedtime is an area of cultural and emotional significance for adults and children alike, in that it poses uncomfortable and difficult questions about the human condition" (p. 26). Darkness, separation, loss of consciousness, and the association between sleep and death all tap into deep feelings and anxieties. One is reminded of the Shakespeare quote: "We are such stuff as dreams are made on; and our little life is rounded with a sleep" (*The Tempest*). In order to relax into sleep, infants and toddlers must relinquish play and the company of parents and friends, and trust that their parents will still be there in the morning.

There are three main ways in which picture books about bedtime deal with these issues. First, many picture books about bedtime present it as a time for play, not for sleep. Examples include *Ten Play Hide-and-Seek* (Dale, 1998), *Can't You Sleep Little Bear* (Waddell & Firth, 1988), and *The Midnight Gang* (Wild & James, 1996). Some picture books deal with bedtime by explaining that all creatures, human and animal, go to sleep. Each page of *Sleepy Book* (Zolotow & Bobri, 1960) presents the sleeping patterns of different animals using poetic language in the timeless present tense. The animals are depicted in muted colours against a dark grey night sky. The last page depicts two sleeping children, with a moon and stars above their heads. This pattern of listing different animals going to sleep is frequently used in picture books for infants and toddlers.

Finally, some picture books deal with bedtime by depicting children carrying out ritual behaviours, such as putting on special clothing (pyjamas), carrying ritual objects (blankets, teddies) and having a bedtime story. The child in *Goodnight Moon* (Brown & Hurd, 1947) engages in ritual behaviour by saying goodnight to the things in his bedroom, and then to the moon and the stars. As he gradually names and farewells these items, the pages grow darker, until the last page shows the child asleep. As Spitz (1999) explains "In Goodnight Moon, the formal structure creates ideal conditions under which children can play out themes concerning the mastery of fears. In Goonight Moon, these fears are mainly of darkness, abandonment, loss of love and of control" (Spitz, 1999, p. 29).

Concluding Remarks

Picture books play a powerful role in shaping young children's growth and development. Parents' and educators' choice of picture books to read to children aged under three is an important one, as the picture book influences the qualities of the adult–child talk surrounding the shared reading, provides entertainment, addresses children's concerns, and influences their attitudes and values. As Stephens (1992) points out, "Picture books can, of course, exist for fun, but they can never be said to exist without either a socializing or educational intention, or else without a specific orientation towards the reality constructed by the society that produces them" (p. 158). Spitz (1999) reflects on the importance of picture books for children's development, "because they are sanctioned by significant adults, they gain ascendency over children's imaginative lives and exert influence well into the future" (p. 208).

References

Ahlberg, J., & Ahlberg, A. (1982). *The baby's catalogue*. Puffin.

Ahlberg, J., & Ahlberg, A. (1983). *Peepo!* Puffin.

Anderson, C. C., & Apseloff, M. F. (1989). *Nonsense literature for children: Aesop to Seuss.* Library Professional Publications.

Apseloff, M. (1987). Books for babies: Learning toys or pre-literature? *Children's Literature Association Quarterly*, 12(2), 63–66. doi:10.1353/ch.0.0382.

de la Bedoyere, C. (2014). *My Little Book of Animals*. QED Publishing.

Bettelheim, B. (1976). *The uses of enchantment: The meaning and importance of fairy tales.* Penguin.

Boynton, S. (2011 [1984]). *Moo, baa, la la la!* Little Simon.

Brown, M. W., & Hurd, C. (1947). *Goodnight moon*. Harper.

Bruner, J. (1986). *Actual minds, possible worlds*. Harvard University Press.

Burningham, J. (1974). *The baby*. Jonathan Cape.

Burningham, J. (1975). *The blanket*. Jonathan Cape.

Burningham, J. (1985). *Alphabet Book*. Walker Books.

Cameron-Faulkner, T., & Noble, C. (2013). A comparison of book text and child directed speech. *First Language*, 33(3), 268–279. doi:10.1177/0142723713487613.

Campbell, J. (1949). *The hero with a thousand faces*. Princeton University Press.

Carle, E. (1969). *The very hungry caterpillar*. Puffin.

Carle, E., & Martin, B. (1997). *Brown bear, brown bear, what do you see?* Penguin.

Chambers, A. (1985). The reader in the book. In *Booktalk: Occasional writing on Literature and Children*. Thimble Press.

Cocks, N. (2004). The implied reader. Response and responsibility: Theories of the implied reader in children's literature criticism. In K. Lesnik-Oberstein (Ed.), *Children's literature* (pp. 93–117). Palgrave Macmillan Publishers.

Cox, T., & Miller, D. (2003). *Snap went Chester*. Hachette.

Dale, P. (1998). *Ten play hide-and-seek*. Walker Books.

Dodd, L. (2002 [1985]). *Hairy Maclary from Donaldon's dairy*. Puffin.

Dunn, C. (2002). Theoretical analysis of a mass media segment: The Wiggles magazine. *Australian Screen Education*, 28, 138–141.

Fox, C. (1993). *At the very edge of the forest: The influence of literature on storytelling by children*. Cassell.

Fox, M., & Vivas, J. (2004 [1983]). *Possum magic*. Omnibus Books.

Golden, J. M., & Gerber, A. (1990). A semiotic perspective of text: The picture story book event. *Journal of Reading Behavior*, 22(3), 203–219.

Griffith, K., & Torr, J. (2003). Playfulness in children's books about bedtime: Ambivalence and subversion in the bedtime story. *Papers: Explorations into Children's Literature*, 13(1), 11–24.

Halliday, M. A. K., & Hasan, R. (1989). *Language, context, and text: Aspects of language in a social-semiotic perspective* (2nd ed.). Oxford University Press.

Hasan, R. (1985). *Linguistics, language and verbal art*. Deakin University Press.

Hutchins, P. (2009 [1967]). *Rosie's walk*. Penguin Random House.

Kiefer, B. (1988). Picture books as contexts for literary, aesthetic, and real world understandings. *Language Arts*, 65(3), 260–271.

Klassen, J. (2011). *I want my hat back*. Candlewick Press.

Lewis, D. (2001). *Reading contemporary picture books*. Routledge. doi:10.4324/9780203354889.

Machin, S., & Vivas, J. (2014 [1989]). *I went walking*. Scholastic.

Mangan, L. (2018). *Bookworm: A memoir of childhood reading.* Vintage.

Maris, R. (1984). *Are you there, Bear?* Puffin.

Martin, H., Simpson, J., & Bowman, A. (2000). *The Book of Animals.* ABC Books.

Meek, M. (1982). *Learning to read.* Bodley Head.

Meek, M. (1988). *How texts teach what readers learn.* Thimble Press.

Montag, J. L. (2019). Differences in sentence complexity in the text of children's picture books and child-directed speech. *First Language,* 39(5), 527–546. doi:10.1177%2F0142723719849996.

Montag, J. L., Jones, M. N., & Smith, L. B. (2015). The words children hear: Picture books and the statistics for language learning. *Psychological Science,* 26(9), 1489–1496. doi:10.1177/0956797615594361.

Nikolajeva, M., & Scott, C. (2000). The dynamics of picturebook communication. *Children's Literature in Education,* 31, 225–239. doi:10.1023/A:1026426902123.

Nodelman, P. (1996). *The pleasures of children's literature* (2nd ed.). Longman.

Nodelman, P., & Reimer, M. (2003). *The pleasures of children's literature* (3rd ed.). Pearson.

Ormerod, J. (2022a [1982]). *Sunshine.* HarperCollins.

Ormerod, J. (2022b [1982]. *Moonshine.* HarperCollins.

Reese, E., & Riordan, J. (2017). Picturebooks and development psychology. In B. Kummerling-Mcibauer (Ed.), *The Routledge companion to picturebooks* (pp. 381–390). Routledge.

Rockwell, A., & Rockwell, H. (1971). *The toolbox.* Hamish Hamilton.

Rosenblatt, L. M. (1982). The literary transaction: Evocation and response. *Theory into Practice,* 21(4), 268–277. www.jstor.org/stable/1476352.

Scott-Mitchell, C. (1987). Further flight: The picture book. In M. Saxby & G. Winch (Eds.), *Give them wings: The experience of children's literature* (pp. 75–90) Macmillan Education Australia.

Sendak, M. (1963/2001). *Where the wild things are.* Penguin.

Shahaeian, A. M., Wang, C., Tucker-Drob, E., Geiger, V., Bus, A. G., & Harrison, L. J. (2018). Early shared reading, socio-economic status, and children's cognitive and school competencies: Six years of longitudinal evidence. *Scientific Studies of Reading,* 22(6), 485–502. doi:10.1080/10888438.2018.1482901.

Simmons, J. (1988). *Come on Daisy!* Orchard Books.

Spitz, E. H. (1999). *Inside picture books.* Yale University Press.

Spufford, F. (2002). *The child that books made: A memoir of childhood and reading.* Faber & Faber.

Stephens, J. (1992). *Language and ideology in children's fiction.* Longman.

Sutton, S., & Lovelock, B. (2008). *Roadworks.* Walker Books.

Torr, J. (2007). The pleasure of recognition: Intertextuality in the talk of preschoolers during shared reading and with mothers and teachers. *Early Years: An InternationaJournal of Research and Development,* 27 (1), 77–93. doi:10.1080/09575140601135163.

Torr, J., & Griffith, K. (2003). An analysis of children's alphabet books: Exploring the role played by nonsense in the construction of meaning between text and implied reader. In J. McKenzie, D. Darnell, & A. Smith (Eds.), *Cinderella transformed: Multiple voices and diverse dialogues in children's literature* (pp. 8–15). University of Canterbury.

Torr, J., & Scott, C. (2006). Learning "special words": technical vocabulary in the talk of adults and pre-schoolers during shared reading. *Journal of Early Childhood Research,* 4 (2), 153–167. doi:10.1177/1476718X06063534.

van Lierop-Debrauwer, H. (2017). Hybridity in picturebooks. In B. Kummerling-Meibauer (Ed.), *The Routledge companion to picturebooks* (pp. 81–90). Routledge.

Waddell, M., & Firth, B. (1988). *Can't you sleep, little bear?* Walker Books.
Watanabe, S., & Ohtomo, Y. (1987). *How do I put it on?* Puffin.
Wild, M., & Brooks, R. (1995). *Old pig.* Allen and Unwin.
Wild, M., & James, A. (1996). *The midnight gang.* Omnibus Books.
Wild, M., & Vivas, J. (1994). *Our granny.* Houghton Mifflin Company.
Zolotow, C., & Bobri, V. (1960). *Sleepy book.* The World's Works.

Index

Note: Page locators in **bold** refer to tables.

For Product Safety Concerns and Information please contact our EU
representative GPSR@taylorandfrancis.com
Taylor & Francis Verlag GmbH, Kaufingerstraße 24, 80331 München, Germany

www.ingramcontent.com/pod-product-compliance
Ingram Content Group UK Ltd.
Pitfield, Milton Keynes, MK11 3LW, UK
UKHW021455080625
459435UK00012B/521